A history

From earliest times

Isaac Newton Lewis

Alpha Editions

This edition published in 2020

ISBN : 9789354013768

Design and Setting By
Alpha Editions
email - alphaedis@gmail.com

A HISTORY

OF

WALPOLE, MASS.

FROM EARLIEST TIMES
WITH ILLUSTRATIONS

BY

ISAAC NEWTON LEWIS, A.M., L.L.B.

Life member of The American Historical Association and The New England Historic-Genealogical Society

PUBLISHED BY THE

First Historical Society of Walpole, Mass.

1905

PREFACE

EVERY town, like every individual, has both character and history. Be it good or bad, some one is interested in it; some one is vitally bound fast to it, either for weal or woe. This grows wider and stronger with a town's age and influence. Our town, though fast forgetting its ancient traditions and sturdy virtues, from its great age, alone, deserves the unselfish efforts of some one of its many children in its preservation and perpetuation. The older the town, the more difficult and meager its earliest history becomes. The following pages, mostly appearing from time to time during the past forty years of my life, in my contributions to newspaper, magazine, and public audiences, I now for the first time in book form offer to my native, though somewhat unworthy town, as a tribute to my departed co-workers of the old First Walpole Historical Society, of which I am now the only surviving member. May its reception be as kind and cordial as the heart of the giver.

ISAAC NEWTON LEWIS.

EAST WALPOLE, MASS.,
June 30, 1905.

TO

MY FATHER AND MOTHER

William and Judith M. Lewis,

TO WHOSE USEFUL, UNSELFISH LIVES

SO MANY HAVE BEEN INDEBTED,

THESE PAGES ARE FILIALLY INSCRIBED.

ILLUSTRATIONS

A HISTORY OF WALPOLE, MASS.

CHAPTER I

THE towns of Dedham and Dorchester, ranging side by side from north to south, with their division line in what is now Walpole territory practically where Washington Street now runs, were among the first municipal corporations of the Province of Massachusetts Bay in America. The former was first called "Contentment," the latter "Dorchester New Grants" or "Graunts beyonde the Blew Hilles." Through this territory ran two old Indian trails, each apparently tending towards Lake Wollomonopoag and other fishing and hunting grounds of the Wampanoag and Narragansett tribes of Indians, of which King Philip afterward became their most famous character and leader.

One of these trails afterward became the "Old Roebuck Road" or "Old Post Road," the other the "Old Saw Mill Road," to the Walpole Common, and from that point to Stop River and King Philip's territory beyond, the old Wrentham Road. These trails were blazed or indicated by burnt marks on the forest trees, and sometimes, either to find a tree or escape some barrier, crooked and turned until they often cast a grave suspicion upon the condition, if not the wisdom, of the original constructor. Even later than 1690 these old ways could be easily traveled only on foot or horseback, and in the latter manner the writer's ancestor, a Dedham constable, tax collector, and tithing man, was obliged to perform his arduous duties from Dedham even to the Wrentham line. His horse survived, however, and, together with a share in a sawmill, is appropriately mentioned in the inventory of his estate. After some years, ox-teams began to undertake these trails, and Dedham, wishing to derive some benefit from the great cedar swamp here, voted in 1658 to lay out the old Sawmill road; Nathaniel Colburn and Peter Woodward being chosen for that purpose.

This road was intended to connect this cedar swamp and a sawmill built on or near the junction of School Meadow Brook and Neponset River by Capt. Eleazer Lusher and Lieut. Joshua Fisher about 1658, with the centre of Dedham.

Under the date of 1661, after a grant by the town to these men, appears in the Dedham records this entry:

"In Refranc to a Highway betwixt the Saw Mill and the Seader Swampe, Capt. Eleazer Lusher and Lieut. Joshua Fisher coming to Town for Paye for Twoe Bridges made by them in that Highwaye, we taking the same into Confideration, find the Comity chosen by the Towne to laye out that High Waye hath ingaged the Towne thirin, we thrfore to issu the same; to the content of the Towne as we confaive, have chofen these three Men here under written mutually by both Partyes, to Vew and Consider and Determin what may bee a Juste Recompense in that cause for them; provided it be payd out of Highwaye worke. The Men chosen are John Haiward, Peter Woodard, John Fayerbank."

This was really a private way needed to conveniently get the timber from the swamp to the sawmill, but as the right to erect the mill and flow the stream was a public grant with reservations in favor of the public, the latter willingly thus aided the promoters.

The first human habitation built by the early settlers in what is now Walpole territory, in all probability, was at or near this old mill, followed by that of James Fales on Spice or Spring Brook, to whom, according to first records, the Indians early became a constant menace and source of danger. Thomas Clap, who married Mary, daughter of Joshua Fisher, one of the original owners of this sawmill, seems to have been the next permanent settler locating near to what is now the corner of Kendall and Main streets, and including in his estate the old town burial ground, which was, after his death, given to the town of Dedham for its present purpose by his son Eleazer, in return for land nearer the sawmill.

"Avril 2d 1705. Itt was likwize putt too ye Voate of ye Prprıters whether thay doe graunte toe Eleazer Clap three Akers off Lande toe bee layd oute toe him bye Sirvayer & ye Commity apoyntd toe laye oute other Landes, prvided sayd Eleazer Clap doe graunt halfe an Aker off Lande in ye Corner off his hom Lott att yt Corner nexte ye Riviere and ye Highe Waye for a Buryal Plas; sayd three Akers off Lande is graantd as abuvfayd toe bee layed oute toe sayd Eleazer joyninge toe his owne Lande att ye Plas cald ye Majours Playne, this is awnserd in ye Afermitif."

Thomas Clap, the father of the above, may have been

buried here on his homestead, as was usual then and is now common in the Southern States, and this may have led the son to make this exchange. Possibly James Fales, Sr., and others of the first generation, also lay there, as this was after the death of the earliest settlers and nearly twenty years before Walpole was set off from the mother town. The spot, like its younger brother on Walpole Plain, is a venerable and interesting place, containing relics of mortal remains over two hundred and fifty years old: those who first braved this then dangerous wilderness, and by labors truly heroic wrested from savage, wild beast, and stubborn soil their meager comforts of life and home, those who sailed away and captured Louisburg, those who marched against their bitter French and Indian foes at Crown Point and the British redcoats of Lexington, Bunker Hill, and through the entire Revolutionary War. French, English, Welsh, Scotch, Huguenot exile, and negro slave, there lie mingled with their mother earth, unknown, unnoticed, and forgotten; magistrates, ministers, military and plain husbandmen on the same humble level, now, and perhaps forever, like their earthly habitations, long since fallen into darkest oblivion. The well-intentioned efforts of the writer for their permanent welfare have never received the attention and coöperation that their unselfishness and perseverance deserve. Much has been accomplished, but much more could be done. The difficulties of beginning have been surmounted. The cross has already been borne. The crown may be yours.

Then came Quinton Stockwell, Caleb Church, Samuel

Parker, Joseph Kingsbury, Joseph Hartshorn, William Robbins, Isaac Bullard, and a few others, settling at or near the plain a half mile or more below the mill.

Probably the earliest records connected with the history of Walpole are the following entries in the early Dedham records:

"12 Mo 18, 1647, Joh Dwite & Fraunceis Chickeringe give notis of their Hopes of a Myne neer certayn Pondes, Aboute 13 Miles from ye Towne soe claymeing ye P'veledge of ye Towne Graunte, it is in or neere ye South Lyne."

In the town orders, closely connected with the covenant of the original settlers of Dedham, a special reference was made to discoveries of metals, and inducements offered to exploration, leading not only to the above, but to the following, two years later:

"Anthony Fifher, Senio & Robt. Crosseman give Notis of thier Difcoverie of a Myne of Mettall. Claymeing ye Prvelidg of ye Towne Order to them thier heyres and Affignes Lyeing above or Westerly of ye Plas wher Naponcet Rivere devide. Pte being on ye Southe Syde of ye Greateste Streame of ye sd Rivere. & is Pt betwixte ye Deviffion of ye sd Streames Lying in Severalle Places theraboute. 26 of 3 mo. 1649."

Thus early the setting up an iron works and sawmill was frequently discussed, but no action taken. The latter mine referred to was probably on Spring Brook, which was early worked, and concerning which conditions and reservations were, down to the present day, inserted in deeds of conveyance of adjoining land. It has been asserted that the first iron cannon made in this country for use in the French and Indian War were molded from this ore.

In 1647 Eleazer Lusher, one of the promoters of our old sawmill, was allowed by special vote to cut cedars near where he afterward stationed the mill.

Long before this Nathaniel Whiting, an ancestor of the writer, had erected a grist-mill on Mother Brook on the creek early dug by the Dedham first settlers for the purpose of getting proper mill power, and which, to this day, has continued to run most of Dedham's manufacturing industries, while the old sawmill near Blackburn's old privilege, and the iron puddle mill near the Diamond Pond, have long since been entirely forgotten.

In 1660 Eleazer Lusher and Joshua Fisher are again referred to thus:

"Libertie is graunted to ye Undertakers of ye Sawe Mille to cutt Grasse for Haye according to their Graunte, att what Seeson they Judge Meete."

The same year appear the following entries concerning the first minister:

"Libertie is graunted to our Reved Pastore to have 20 acres of his Divident layed out somwher neer ye Sawe Mille to bee layed out by Nath Coalburne and Rich Ellice." "Graunted to Mr Allin Pastore Libertie to take 5 akers off Uplande neere ye Sawe Mille in pt off his Rite in ye Divident of ye 500 Akers and allsoe 5 Akers more there in fulle satiffactione for ye UppLande due for purchafed Lande."

A school had early been established, as appears from the following:

"At a Generall Meting of ye Towne ye 5 of ye 11 mo 1656, ye Towne by Voate give a Calle to Mich. Meatcalfe to keepe Schoole in our Towne and leave it to ye next Selectmen to agree with hym there in."

The following records also refer to our territory:

"Ye Towne bye Voate resolve yt the Swampe neere Meadfield shall bee disposed of in Propriatie.

"Graunted to Daniel Morse two Seders to make Clabbord out in ye above mentioned Swampe.

"Agreed that thofe yt hav felled Trees allready in yt Swampe shall bee caled to Accounte, to make Sattiffacton accordin to Justis. Itt is ordered yt ye Swampe above mentoned shall bee disposed off bye pticuler Graunte to each Townesman according to ye ordinarie Ruls by which Landes have been divided, provided yt noe other Parte therof bee layed out but only such as shall bee ufeful for Ceder Timbur & shall bee Judged meete to bee in Propriatie by ye Men heere after deputed to order ye Same in yt Respecte to whofe Judgement in this Cafe ye Towne promise to submitt Nath Coalburne, Sergt. Fisher & Joshua Fisher are deputted & impowered therin."

This was followed a year later by this entry:

"Att a Generall Meting off ye Inhabatance off ye Towne of Deadham, ye 4 of ye 11 mo 1657. In Refferans to ye Proppofition aboute ye Sawe Mille ye Towne leve ye Anfur till furder Confideration."

The next year

"att a Generalle Metinge of ye Towne 3, 11, 1658. In Refferans to ye Settinge upp off a Sawe Mille, it is lefte to ye men heereafter named to agree & conclude on ye Townes Behalfe with such Pfons as shalle prfent Themfelves for ye Settinge upp off a Sawe Mille & toe give them such Incoragemente as they shall Judge Meete, these three Men are chosen bye ye Towne & if Anny of ye Three apeere to bee sd Pties, then ye Elder is toe bee one of Three & ye Firft Three are Sergt Fifher, Nath Coaleburne, Pet Woodard. Articles refpecting ye Sawe Mille agreed and concluded uppon betwixt ye Comittee deputed by Towne order therunto ye one Ptie & Lieft. Joshua Fifher and Eleazer Lusher who presented to undertake ye Buildinge and Manageing such a Mille on the other Ptie as followeth viz. In Prms: Wee ye sayd Comittee whose Names are heere unto subscribed in ye Name of ye Towne of Deadham and bye ye Truste and Power Towne orders to us in this Case given, give and graunt Libertie unto ye sd Eleazer and Joshua theyer Heyres Executers Administraters and Assignes joyntly & severallie toe builde and erecte a Sawe Mille uppon Naponcett River or any Parte there of wher they shalle Judge most Meete for ye Empvnt off ye Timbur in ye Ceader Swampe allready graunted, and to that Ende to take and make use of eny Timbur whatsoeever, as allso Woode, Stons or Earthe as they shall have Occasine to make use off aboute Buildinge or otherwize as shall apeare nessarie thereunto, all which they have to take in eny Comon Lande of ye Towne, with ye free Use of Soe much in all Respects, aboute sd Mille as they shall occasionallie use for their Worke, and all these to have use and enjoye without Disterbans or Molestation, soe long as themselves or their Heyers or Assignes shall mayntain a Sawe Mille there. And furder whereas ye Charge of Erecting ye Mille aforesd is like to bee Greate, We ye Comittee aforesd, doe for ye incoragemente of ye sd Undertakeres and their Heyeres aforesd, graunte all ye Timbur of alle or eny Kinde or Sorte that shall bee founde eny wheres not formerly graunted, excepting Allwayes that Seder Timbur att ye Southe Ende off ye greate Ceader Swampe aforesd, which we reserve in ye Townes Behalfe yt if ye Towne shall within ye Spase of Twoe Yeares next insewing graunte ye same to such as whose Lottes in ye sd Swampe graunted was defective, for Repairations ther unto or otherwize, we graunt that lote there to ye Undertakers and their Heyers aforesd, allsoe furder that if eny other Swampe shall bee founde within ye foresayd Plas conteyne Twentie Akers of Swampe in one Plase soe that it shall bee Judged bye ye Towne fitt to devide for devident it shall bee encluded in ye former Graunte above written, pvided allwayes that ye Graunte off Timbur aforesd shall not prjudise ye Iron Workes in Case ye Towne shalle pceede therein, nor hinder eny Townsman of Libertie to make use off eny oake Timbur there that for his Use hee shall neede; Allsoe pvided that this Graunte off other Timbur, besids Pine and Ceader shall only extende to such Timbur as is beyonde ye mille & furthere from this Towne than ye sayd Mille. And all these Grauntes abovesd shall remayne and stande good to ye sd Granteese and their Heyers aforesaid soe long as they shall mayntayne a Sawe Mille as aforesaide there. And furder it is agreed, yt in Cafe ye Towne shall laye out a Generall Devident, then it shall bee att ye Libertie of ye sd Undertakers, their Heyers and Affignes aforesd to have their Devident layed out there aboute wher they shall chuse. 2. And futher we ye sayd Comittie doe graunt Libertie to ye sayd Undertakers and their Heyers aforefayd to take yearely soe much Graffe in some Meadowe or Meadowes there-about as shall be sufficient well to winter foure or sixe Oxen, and if Plentie of Meadowe shall be founde there aboute this Graunte shall bee inlarged. 3. We ye Comittie aforesd, doe in ye Behalfe and in ye Name of ye Towne pmise and ingage that noe other sawe mille shall be errected or sett up in or uppon that Streame of Naponcett, except it bee by ye Consente of ye sd Undertakers, for ye Spase of Tenne Yeares after ye Daye of ye Date heere of, that is to saye within ye Bowndes of Deadham. 4. Further it is joyntly agreed that whatsoever Pyne or Ceader Timbur ye sd Mille shall cutt for eny off ye Inhabitanc of this Towne into Inch Boarde, yt one Halfe of ye Boarde shall bee alowed to ye Owners of ye Timber, and ye Refte to ye Owners off ye Mille. And its allsoe agreed that if ye Mille bee at Worke in cutting for ye Owners off ye Mille, and that eny Inhabitant bring a considerabel Quantytie of Tymber to bee cutt, that then ye Mille shall not worke above Tenn Days for ye Owners, before that Tymber of ye sd Inhabi-tent is began to bee cutt, if it bee desired so to bee, and its allso agreed that ye Tymber shall be cutt according to Succeffion of Tyme as it is brot to Mille. And its allso further agreed that if any Inhabitent shall att any Tyme bring so much Tymber that it is a pjudice to ye Owners or Others, then upon Complaynt to ye Select Men for the Tyme being the Select Men shall have Power to regulate ye same as they shall Judge Meete and Equall. 5. Further it is allso agreed, that if eny Man shall have Boarde cutt att ye Mille shall sell eny Board at a lower Price than ye Owners usually doe, then its at the Libertie of ye Owners whether they shall cutt eny more for that Pson for ye Space of two Yeares after or not, but if after ye Mille have been in Worke two Yeares, any such first offer ye sd Boarde to ye Owners at such a Price as is tendered them & that ye Owners aforefd refuse it, then ye sd Psons shall be at Libertie to sell as they se Cause, and all these Graunts Conclufions and Agreemts shall remayne in Fource all ye Tyme that ye saide Sawe Mille shall be mayntayned upon ye sayd Streame. Mrd that all these Graunts above written are made upon this further condicion that ye sd Undertakers, their Heyers, Executors or Affignees, doe erecte and fitt ye sd Mille for Worke before ye 24th of ye 4th month Anno 1660 — subscribed by us ye 4th of March 1658-9."

Next to the old sawmill, the location of the premises of Joseph Hartshorn becomes most important, as both are often mentioned in Dedham's early records in relation to the old grants to the first settlers under the name of the Sawmill dividends. These premises were between the Stetson privilege and Gould Street, and extended from the Neponset River to the waste land to the west, as will later appear.

In the Dedham records we find the following, plainly showing that in those early days men were no more prompt than now in highway matters:

"february 22, 170$\frac{2}{3}$. Upon the Complaynt by the sirveiers that the Waye from the old Saw Mill to the Seder Swamp and to the Meadows is not layd out, the Selectmen have chose Daniel Fisher & John Deane a Comity to laye out said Waye."

Three years passed before this "Comity" reported, and then as follows:

"We whose Names are hereunto fubfcribed, being Deputed by the Towne and Selectmen of Dedham to laye out a High Waye from the Countrie Roade to the old Sawe Mille, and from thence to the greate Seder Swampe beyond said mill, doe make Return of our Doing thereof. We began betweene the House of John Farringtun and the House of (Lieut.) Barachiah Lewis at the Place caled Mackenabs Spring, laying the Waye two Rodes wide as it is now drawn untill it come over the Brooke and then turning to the Right Hand by the Side of the Hille till we Come to the Top of the Hille, and then turning to the left Hande to the Fence of said Lewis, and soe two Rodes wide by the Fence as it now standeth untill we came to the Land of Nathaniel Farringtun, and soe by his Line untill we Come to the Toppe of the Hille by said Farringtuns Field and thus taking in both Wayes as they are now drawn to the Bottom of the Hille, and soe two Rodes wide as the Waye is now most Convenient untill we Come to the Brooke neer the House of Joseph Hartshorne, and then goeing strait up the Hille beyond the Brooke to the Waye old drawn, which Parceill of Waye said Hartshorne doe ingage to make good at his own Charge, if not, as the Waye is now drawn, and so two Rodes wide as the Waye is now drawn to the House of Thomas Clape deceased, and soe runing over Naponset River in the old Wrentham Roade, and soe as the Waye is drawn, to the greate Shaving Plase at the Seder Swampe.

"DANIEL FISHER.
"JOHN DEANE."

The Sawmill road was for more than a hundred years called by its old name and can even now easily be identified its entire length from Dedham, up through Wild Cat, the Hartshorn neighborhood to the old Thomas Clap place, up by the place of his son Thomas, winding around the south side of the hilltop across the centre of what is now the Common, through the river and up Spring Street in a winding course to the plain by the cedar swamp of to-day; but although then called and afterwards known as the Sawmill road, one is disappointed in not finding any indication of where or how it reached that old sawmill institution.

As early as 1700, Ebenezer Fales transported over it the boards to enlarge Dedham's second meeting-house, but in what way he reached the road from the mill is not very clear. It probably was up the hill in the rear of the Blackburn house, over the top of the hill and down its west side, straight across the middle of the Common to where Main Street now bisects the Common.

Under the date of April 2, 1705, the Dedham records make further reference to this old way, as follows:

> "Said Selectmen chose Capt. Samuel Guild and (Lieut.) Barachiah Lewis a Commity to laye out a Highway from the old Saw Mill Roade near four mile Tree to the Country Road at Naponset River."

This was probably Guild Street, Norwood.

In June, 1722, the old Wrentham road or trail which wound from the middle of the Common down over the Neponset River, up over Scratch Hollow, and Powder House Hill to Stop River, was further laid out and improved under the title of "Roade from Thos. Clap's to Stop River two Rodes wide by Jon. Metcalf, Ebenezer Woodard and Jeremiah Fisher."

It is not until Nov. 7, 1723, that we get any clear idea how the northerly connection of the old sawmill and the old Sawmill road was to run. For more than eighty years those patronizing the mill had to take whatever way the Claps and Faleses made use of straight through the Common, all Clap land, or the old Sawmill dividend right of way which was in worse condition. On that date the following report was made:

> "We, the Subscribers being desired by the Selectmen to lay out a High Waye from the Road leading from Wrentham, near the House of Thomas Clap, have attended said Worke and layd out the Waye two Rodes broad near where the Waye is now drawn by the House of Joshua

LONG BEFORE WALPOLE WAS, I WAS

The home of Peter and Abigail Fales, on the west side of Main Street, Walpole Centre, built, probably, in 1690 and from 1732 to 1778 the parsonage of the Rev. Phillips Payson, Sr. Taken down a few years ago to make way for a new house by Dr. French

Clap, and soe over the River near the old Saw Mille, and as the Waye now is to Claps Meadows, and soe over the River and the South end of the Meadow called brush Meadow into the Land of Robert Allin, and soe to Dorchester Line, and in the Land of John Allin next to Dorchester Line to the thirteenth Lott.

PETER FALES,
JOSHUA CLAP."

The Thomas Clap mentioned was son of the Thomas before referred to, and lived in a house given him by his father and represented to have been bought of Colonel Byfield, which stood near the Lewis Clap place. He had considerable of his father's property; gave to Walpole, soon after its seceding from Dedham and incorporation, its first pound. He also, sad to relate, was the first taxpayer punished for giving a false return of his taxable property, and was obliged to pay a fine which went to the poor of the town.

The Joshua Clap mentioned was his brother, lived near the Warren Clap place, and boarded Walpole's first minister, the Rev. Joseph Belcher.

Peter Fales, the other committee, lived on the farm north of Spring Brook, which some ten years after became the parsonage of Walpole's second minister, the Rev. Phillips Payson.

This old way from the Sawmill road to the land beyond the sawmill, after the ascent of the old Dam hill from the Common, connected with a way across the Dorchester line to Colonel Billing's farm in what is now Sharon, passing by the house of James Bardens, one of the first members of the Walpole church.

The only other road of that early period was from

the Neponset River at what is now Lewis Corner, and on through the Sawmill Dividends to the old sawmill. North and High streets were not made for years after.

The Wampanoags claimed all the land south of Stop River, and before Dedham could settle what is now Wrentham, she was obliged to send a commission to King Philip at Lake Wollomonopoag to treat with him for the adjoining territory.

Under 9, 8, 1669, their appears this action in the matter:

"Upon notis frome Phillip Sagamor yt hee is nowe att Wollomonuppoage and offeres a Treatie aboute a sayl off his Rites in ye Landes thereaboute within ower Bowndes nott yt puchafd in Confiderashun tharoff Tymo. Dwite Anth. Fisher Junr. Robt Ware Rich Ellice and Jon Thirston Senr. or any Foure or Three off them are deputid and empourd toe repayre toe Wollomonuppoag on ye Morrowe, and Treet with ye sd Phillip in Ordere toe a Contrak with him toe cleere alle his remayneing Rites within our towne Bowndes pvided hee make his Rite apeere, and uppon Contrak secur our Towne from all Claymes off alle other Endiens in ye Landes hee contrak for, uppon which Tearmes and what els this Comittie or ye majour pt off them shalle Juge requisit if they se Juste Corse toe make a Contrak with him, thay have Pour soe to doe, and make Retourn to ye Select Men off wt thay doe heerein lesse or more.

"A Bil is given Samll Fisher toe Receive off yt Cunftabel 12 s in fulle Sattyffaxun for his Charj in Entertayneing ye Endeans in ye Tyme off Treetie aboute ye purchifing thayr Rites att Wollomonuppoag and ye Reste off ye Lande within oure Bowndes.

"Upon Reseate off a Lettr fro Sagarmoor Phillip off Mownt hope tendring Sal off his Rites in ye Landes in oure Towne beyonde Wollomonuppoag and thereaboute, and desyringe 5£ in peage att pfent, uppon yt accont a Lettr is ordered toe bee ritten and sent toe Nathenll Payen off Rehoobothe toe difburfe yt fom for ye Towne toe ye sayd Sagermoor uppon Condiciuns as in yt Lettr exprest. In reffrans toe ye Quefton concerninge ye Endiens empruving Land att Wollomonuppoag itt is Jugd mete toe sende them a copye off ye Graunte mad toe Indien Sarah and ye Condishians thar off and thayer Ackeeptanc thereoff yt if thay have Libertie toe emprove itt thys sumer, thay may knoe itt is Curtsy and expeck itt noe longere."

In 1684 we find the following record:

"4, 16, 84 Affembld after Trayninge Enfin Fullar, Sargt Ponde, Sergt Metcalfe, Sergt Ellic, Nath Stearnes.

"Wee being infomed yt Jofias Sonn ye Indian Sacham laye Claym toe yt Tracte off Lande Lyeing between Dorchestar Lyne and Naponcett Rivier neer aboute ye Sawe Mille and yt hee mak Teander off ye sayd Track toe sale; wee doe tharfore desyre and apoynte Sergt Rich Ellic toe Surch ye Rekords, and see iff eny Thyng maye bee fourde toe clere Deadhams Tytel toe ye sd Lande and make Retourne att ye fyrft Opertunitie."

As late as 1682 we find

"upon Infourmashun yt ther ar sevrall Indianes resideinge in our Towne toe ye Offenc and Damiage off Some off our Inhabitanc. A Warrante is sente toe ye Counstapel toe warne tham toe remuve themfelves toe Puncapogue, Natik or Wemesett acordyng toe Lawe."

It is interesting to note the many and momentous questions and undertakings of that struggling Dedham community. The very month when it is trying to pacify the savage, we find the following reference to its worthy effort to help on the only seat of learning in the English settlements in America, called, but a few years before, after the Rev. John Harvard, of Charlestown, Mass., Harvard College.

"In Ansser toe ye Cort Ordere sente upp toe ye Towne toe demaunde ye Remayndr off ye Paie yt is toe bee payd yt was givn toe ye new Collidg;

wee choos Capt Fisher toe goe toe Boston toe give an Acounte toe Comity accordynge toe ye Corte Ordere howe Thinges doe yett stande."

If the payment was to be in coin, we can easily see their difficulty. When they were forced to negotiate with the Indian chief Nahoiden that same year, the best they could do was ten pounds in money, and the remainder in Indian corn and land far removed. What little coin there was was clipped and of short weight. The common purse in use was the meal bag in which went Indian corn, peas, rye and sometimes wampum or peag, as it was called, and not infrequently iron nails. Minister, schoolmaster and strong water keeper were all served alike, fire-wood and cedar rails notwithstanding.

Dedham had already made two purchases of title from Indians, one of which had come from Wampituck, sachem of the Neponset and Punkapoag tribes, who claimed pretty much, if not all, of Walpole territory. In the deed taken to satisfy the above claim of Josiah, a reservation was made to the tribe of Punkapoag Indians of all the land between the angle made by the Neponset River and Dorchester line and old Lewis Lane, now the southerly end of Plimpton Street, for hunting, trapping, and fishing. Old relics still exist of this late Indian use, and doubtless close exploration would disclose many Indian remains. They clung to this reservation, greatly to the annoyance of James Fales and the very few settlers thereabout, until their chief, on October 8, 1685, was induced to relinquish his rights in the following manner:

"To all People to whom these Presents shall come, Charles Josiah, son of Josiah, son and Heir of Chicatawbut only Sachem of the Massachusetts Country and sole Proprietor thereof when the English arrived in these Parts, sendeth Greeting; Know Ye that in a late Sale of the Towne of Dedham to the Inhabitants thereof, I reserved to myself two Hundred Acres of land, and to my Heires and Affigns to be layd out near Naponsett River, neare the Sawe Mill of sayd Towne, which is since conveniently layd out as is there covenanted and agreed, reference thereto being had; Now be it known that I, the sayd Charles Josiah, Sachem in Consideration of a valuable Some of Monie to be in hand payd by Nathaniel Paige of Boston, with the Advice and Confent and Knowledge and Approbation of William Stoughton of Dorchester, Esq. and Joseph Dudley of Roxbury, Esq. my Guardian and Prochien ami, have given, granted, bargained, sold, aliened, set over, enfeofed, and confirmed unto him, the sayd Nathaniel Paige, alle my Right, Title and Interest in and to the sayd Land by me reserved and survaied as aforefaid lyeing, situate and being in the Boundes of the aforefayd Towne of Dedham contayning by Estimation Two Hundred Acres, bee the same more or lesse, butted and bounded by the Line betwix the Townes of Dorchester and Roxbury on the Southward and on all other Sides by the Common and undisposed Lands of the sayd Towne of Dedham or however otherwise butted and bounded. To have and to hold, possess and enjoy the whole aforefayd Tract of Land contayning and bounded as aforefayd. In Witnefs whereof I, the sayd Charles Josiah, have hereunto sett my Hand and seale, this eighth of October Anno Dom. One thousand Sixe Hundred Eighty and Five.

"CHARLES JOSIAH (*Signum*).

"WILLIAM STOUGHTON.
"JOSEPH DUDLEY."

The last Indians in Dedham territory were Alexander Quabish and his wife Sarah David. The latter died at Joseph Wight's in 1774. Thus by this deed which was long after found in an old Salem desk and restored to Dedham, the town was, with the exception of the Indian Sarah and George and Ephraim, who continued to plant a little Indian corn and catch a few rabbits and fish, quite rid of permanent aboriginal rovers.

This was for years called Paige's Farm and extended from the School Farm of Dorchester Grant of 1662, which came up to the office of F. W. Bird & Son, to old Lewis Lane, now East Plimpton Street, and was found to exceed the 200 acres mentioned. Nathaniel Paige was a public marshal, and left on his death two daughters, Elizabeth and Sarah. Elizabeth married John Simpkins, mariner, who with Thomas Simpkins, cooper, of Boston, sold the northerly half of the farm, 102 acres, Sept. 16, 1732, to Thomas Pemberton, mariner, of Boston, who some years later sold a portion to the Pettee family, members of which still live on a part of the premises; a part also was owned by Isaac Lewis, Sr., and his brother John.

Sarah, the other daughter of Paige, married Samuel Hill, Jr., of Boston and Billerica, who sold the southerly portion of the farm, 102 acres, May 12, 1725, to Joseph Carroll of Stoughton and Samuel Foster of Salem, the deed reciting that the other half was owned by Mr. John Simpkins of Boston, mariner, and that the premises were bounded on the south in part by land of Thomas Paine (the Second Sawmill dividend) and in part by land of Thomas Metcalf (the Third Sawmill dividend), west and northwest by Neponset River, and east and southeast by Dorchester line. In 1736, Carroll and Foster made an equal division of their half of the farm by a deed still in the author's possession, Carroll taking the easterly half afterwards owned by Isaac Lewis, Jr., and Foster the westerly half, which, not long after, was sold to Joseph

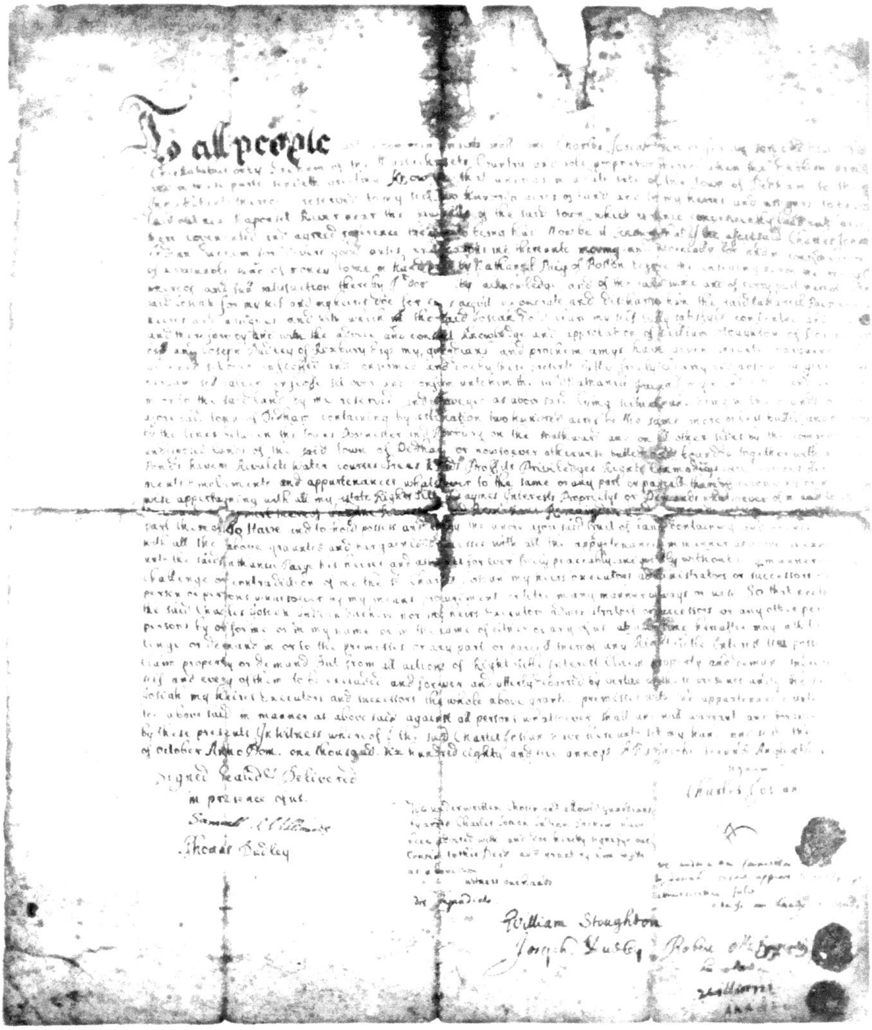

THE OLD INDIAN DEED OF THE ISAAC LEWIS, ELEAZER RHOADS, SAMUEL THOMPSON, AND JOSEPH PETTEE FARMS IN EAST WALPOLE, OTHERWISE CALLED PAIGE'S FARM, REDUCED TO ONE TENTH OF ITS ACTUAL SIZE

It contains the names of two Governors of the Province, and was the last purchase and covered the last hunting grounds of the Indian in our territory. The old Indian mortar near the Neponset in Plimptonville is of the same period

LEWIS CORNER, EAST WALPOLE

Old Lewis Lane, birthplace of John W. Lewis, East Street. Line between Paige's farm and the First and Second Sawmill dividends. Scene of the last parade of the old Walpole Light Infantry. The William Lewis place and birthplace of the writer

Coney, who in 1773, sold it to Isaac Lewis, Sr., a portion of which premises still remains in the hands of his descendants, although the extreme westerly border, for years known as Lewis Lane, was sold by him to Levi Maxey, agent of the Neponset Factory Company, for a way to their mills, the deed being drawn in 1814 to William Appleton, of Boston, who held an interest in the mills.

The older towns of the Province of Massachusetts Bay apportioned their common lands among their inhabitants according to their claims and means, and so Dedham and Dorchester before 1700 began to assign to settlers portions of the territory now belonging to Walpole. There was a long and narrow stretch of waste land bounded on the north by this old Paige Farm, on the east by the old Dorchester line, and on the west by the Neponset River, which was known as the Common land between the sawmill and land of Joseph Hartshorn, and the Dorchester line.

Portions of this were soon coveted by the few settlers in this part of Dedham, and in compliance with their wishes, the town voted to divide it among the settlers and its other inhabitants. Thus before 1720 the whole of this new section was taken up. The lots, or Sawmill Dividends as they were, until recent years, commonly called, began at what used to be the Daniel Ellis factory, afterward machine shop of C. G. & H. M. Plimpton, which was lot One. Lot Two was assigned to Thomas Paine, who, like most of the first owners, never made any use of it. Lot Three fell to Thomas Metcalf, which, with the Paine lot, soon became the property of Joseph Coney, and William and Joseph Pettee, and, finally, in 1768 and subsequently, except the east side of the way, the property of John Lewis, an old soldier of the French and Indian war, and elder son of Isaac Lewis, owner of the lot beyond. The Fourth lot fell to Sergt. Eleazer Kingsbury, who, with his heirs, held it for twenty years, and then sold to Isaac Lewis, son of Lieut. Barachiah Lewis, whose descendants still retain it. This Fourth lot contains some sixty odd acres, and was the first sawmill dividend to extend the whole distance from the Neponset River to the Dorchester line. Thus were these Dividends continued southward up to and beyond the Common until the sawmill and cedar swamp were reached, and through their whole course, from the upper part of Bird's Pond to the junction of Common and Washington streets, was reserved a right of way for the several owners to pass and repass, the Lewis Lane, before referred to, extending to what is now East Street. (East and Union streets from the old country or Post road at the old Isaac Lewis place, afterwards Warren Fairbanks place, in East Walpole, were not laid out for many years.) East Street from Lewis's corner to Allen's corner, thence over Fales and Allen and other lands to the sawmill and Dorchester line.

The entire way was in its original bad condition until ten years after Walpole separated from Dedham, and no worthy attempt to make even the old Sawmill Road, our chief street, fairly passable was made by Dedham until the year of the final struggle for separation from the mother town. Highways in those days were, like taxes, when possible, worked out, and disposition was generally as weak and profitless as the labor expended.

The patient oxen of our fathers perseveringly, though often disastrously, like the Indian, overcame all difficulties; so until the town was pretty clear from the Indian title, no widening or leveling of roads was attempted. Even in his most peaceable condition, the Indian, although the early settlers often took for help one or more of the young men into their families, was nevertheless sharply watched, and usually avoided.

"In 1660 Dedham voted that Lieut. Fisher, Ens. Fisher, Sergt Fuller, Sergt Ellice Rich Wheeler are deputied to viewe ye Lande both Upp Lande and Medowe neere aboute ye Pondes by Gorge Indiand Wigg-warm & make Reporte of what they finde to ye Select Men in ye firſt Optunitie they can take."

Also, during the same year, it was voted as follows:

"Lieft Fisher & Sergt Ellice air deputed to Treate (& if it may bee) to conclud wth ye Indians or Sagamour that clayme Rite att Wolo-monuppucke to bye them all oute and cleere ye Plas from all Endian Tytel."

In 1667 it was voted that

"A Lettr is odered to bee sent to Capt Willett to requeaste him to bee helpfull to us bye speakeing wth Sagamor Phillip to cause ye Endiens to departe from Wollomonuppoage."

The next year it was voted,

"Upon ye Requeaste of Endian Sarah of Wollomonuppoage moved in her Beehalfe to ye ppriate ther soe many of them as are preſent doe Graunte to ye saide Endian Sarah one piece off Upp Lande neere a

Ponde aboute 2 Miles west warde from ye scituation of ye Towneshipp at Wollomonuppoag in exchange for that Lande ye sayd Sarah here sonne, or Gorge her Bruther possesse or Clayme in ye Towneſhippe aforeſayd to bee sett out to her bye Robt Ware and Saml Fisher ye field beinge by estimation 10 Akers and ye have Libertie to take Fenceing Stuffe and are injoyned to keepe it sufficentlie fensed."

This George was the same mentioned above. For years he and his sister Sarah had planted maize upon several plains between Stop River and Archer's Pond. Other Indians, besides the friendly native settlement, well known to our ancestors, were Chicatabut, Ephraim, John Monaco, Nahatan, John Magus, John Speene, Charles Josias alias Wampituck, Mayns, Nowanitt, Peter and Thomas Speene, Waban, King Philip, Wampituck and Ogquonikongquamesitt. Some were useful in running errands and freeing the forests and swamps of the wolves and other troublesome wild beasts, others as counter-irritants against the common hardships and perplexities of daily life. Chicatabut married the daughter of Wampituck, and was the father of Josias.

As early as 1637 we find:

"Ordered ye watches & Wardes shall bee carefully sett & kept & alle othere Thyngs done & performed accordinge to ye Ordere of ye Towne in ye best Manner we may bee abel. And to yt Perpose Daniell Moss chosen Sarjant att Armes to order ye same untill we have other supplie."

CHAPTER II

THE names of the early settlers here were variously spelled; thus we read that Dedham in 1663 entered in her records:

"Graunted unto James Vales a perceil of Lande att ye easte ende of ye Lands hee have att ye Sawe Mille in sattiffaxtion for his purchis Lande that was due to ye halfe Lott he live uppon, as it shall bee layd out by Jofhua Fisher & Edwarde Richardes."

Immediately after comes the following reference to our present Common:

"Graunted unto Mr. John Allin 18 Akers off Lande uppon ye Playne halfe a mille this sid ye Sawe Mille on this sid ye Brooke on ye righte Hand of ye Parth as wee goe to ye Mille."

And this is followed in the same year by reference to the meadow on the Neponset, above the mill, as follows:

"2d. Agreed to perpose to ye Towne that all comon meadowes of ye Towne not formerlie stayted shall be layd out in a generall Devident and ye Meadowe aboute ye Sawe Mille that is not formerlie stayted to bee solde to ye ppriaters that are & shall bee setled aboute ye Sawe Mille."

At this early date, the greater portion of this part of Dedham was held in common, so we in the same year find the town recorded:

"Upon ye Requeast of Samuell Parker and Thomas clape to have

Libertie to cutt sume Grase not withstandinge ye Order of Reyſtraynt to cutt in ye comon medowes, Libertie is graunted them to cutt 6 Lodes, Sam Parker 4 Lods, Tho Clape 2 Lods provid thay cutt not neearer ye Towne then ye Sawe Mille nor in ye Graunte mayd in Referanc to ye Sawe Mille."

The same year, the same Samuel Parker obtained the following grant, which mentions Spring Brook under its early name:

"Samuel Parker movinge for a parcell of Swampie Lande betwene Spice brooke & ye Lande hee Bot of Joshua Fisher, ye Moshun being putt to Voat. Ye Voat was Generall for ye Graunt off ye Moshun, ye Contrarie beinge putt not Eny voated ye Contrarie."

Just before this stands a reference to the old Plain or Wrentham road (not the Honey Pot road):

"Joshua Kent Robt. Ware & Sergt Ellice beeing Defective in ther High Waye Worke this yeare, thay have Libertie to doe so much Worke in ye High Waye ledeing to Woolomonapock as thay were behindhande this laſt Sumer, which if thay doe, ye Towne doe acquitt them."

The following year we find another reference to this old road, and, it would seem, to the second mill, within well authenticated history, built in Dedham as a grist-mill:

"Graunted to Daniel Ponde and Ezra Morse a Rocke Stun intendid for a Mille Stun, and suposed capibel thereof, lyeing aboute 6 Rodd easte frum Stopp River, and neere ye Parth that leade to Wolomunuppag, for ye Uſe off ye Mille now inteendid to be builte."

This mill was thought necessary on account of alleged dissatisfaction with Nathaniel Whiting, owner of the old mill below the proposed new site. The stream on which these mills stood was an artificial one dug by the early settlers in accordance with the following vote:

"3 of 11 mo 1652. Libertie is graunted to cutt a Creeke or Ditche thro eny Comon Lande of ye Towne which shall bee occasioned bye ye Cuttinge ye same thro Broad Meedowe from Rivere to Rivere."

This creek is called the very next year Mother Brook, and is so known to this day. It united the Charles River with the Neponset below. As early as 1640, however, mention is made of a mill brook and pond as well as Vine Brook.

As early as 1653 our well-known stream, Stop River, is referred to in this record, for to its meadows, as well as to those in the south part of the town, Dedham early drove its cattle to pasture.

"Graunted unto Willm Averey & his Heyers forever, one Peell of Meedowe conteyning aboute 4 or 5 Akers, abuttinge upon and adjoyneing Stopp Rivere neere Meadfield & in Pt upon Nath Coalburrs Meedowe & upon Meedfield Lyne & ye Waste Upplande."

Three years later it has another mention thus:

"Graunted to ye Widdowe Morse of Meatfild to take in sume smale Parcell of Uppe Land within ye Fense for ye strayninge of ye Lynes to Fense in ye Medowe bot bye Joseph Morse off Sergt Averey neere Stope Rivere."

The Neponset River is mentioned as early as 1639, three years after the grant for the settlement of Dedham, where it is called Naponcet and represented as having a mill belonging to "Ye Worshful Mr Israell Stoughton of Dorchester," whose farm covered a portion of the easterly part of Dedham.

Again in 1649 is found another mention, with the same spelling, and applying to the river in the centre of what is now Walpole. As late as 1794, this river was represented as dividing just above the Brook (Spice or Spring Brook) into a north and south fork, what is now called Mill Brook being the former. In fact it seems that both of these streams were once or twice miscalled "brookes." Stop River on Walpole Plain, however, from the very earliest has preserved its name and identity.

The origin of its name is unknown. It may have been so called because it, as the division line between the Wampanoag and Massachusetts Indians, formed a stop or fixed boundary.

But there were in those early days other pests besides the Indian. Medfield had been set off into a separate town in 1651, Wrentham in 1661. As early as 1649 appears the following reference to the former:

"Eleazer Lusher is deputied on Behaf of ye Towne of Deadham to afist in Layinge out ye Farme graunted to Mr Edward Aleyne, deceafd, wch is toe bee layd oute att Bogastowe now called Meadfild,"

and to the latter,

"Deadham 21, 8 mo, 1661. Ye Towne beinge caled toegeather bye ye Select Men voated as foloweth: Firft yt ye Bownds of ye Plantacion intended att ye Plas caled Woollomonpuck shall bee East Worde uppon ye Rivier caled Stoope Riviur beginyng att Meadfild Bowndes and soe all alonge as yt Rivier upp Streeme ly till itt bee aboute Halfe a Mille above ye Falles in yt Rivier wheare aboute ye Parthe to ye sd Plas ly and from thence Southe ward to Dorchester Lyne."

In 1670 our first settler James Fales was chosen surveyor of the latter and called "Surveyer for ye Fammilyes att ye Sawe Mille and Wollomonuppoage."

All the country around was infested with wildcats, rattlesnakes, foxes, bears, and wolves. Even King Philip, as though the settlers had not quite enough to bear, had begun to vex the settlers, so we find:

"Att a Generall Towne Meeteing 2, 11, 1670 ye fyrft Cas ppounded refpectynge ye Cleereing ye Queston of Tytel purchafd off Sagamore Phillip and ye payemt for ye same is lefft to ye Care and Discreton of ye Seleect Men this Daye to bee chusen to doe therein as thay shalle aprhend ye Cas may requir."

Wolf pits and deer hedges were so well known as to not infrequently serve as localities and boundaries, and when an exceedingly annoying tax or assessment came to be demanded from the settler, he seized his old matchlock, and wore away his feelings stalking the plentiful game, from which diversion he generally returned with the wherewithal to meet the constable. For Dedham as early as 1639 passed the following vote:

"Ordered yt whoesoever off our Towne shall kille a Woolfe wth in or neere our Towne shall have payd unto him Tenn Shilling toe bee Raysd uppon ye Hede off evry Beeste yt is kepte wthin our sayd Towne."

This became in 1647 ten shillings from the town and ten from the "Countrie," twenty shillings a head, and hunting for wolves immediately became as irresistible as keeping public house or seizing a public office. Accordingly, we find in 1651:

"Antho. Fisher, Jr. Joh. Fayerbanks, Rich Ellice Jonath. Fayerbanks ar bye ye Towne deputeid to Attende uppon ye Worke off Takeing

Wolfes & ar apoynted to receave Tenn Shilling for eache Wolfe thay shall kill above wt ye Courte order doe apoynt & pvided yt ye sayd Wolfes may bee mayd apeare to bee killd within 3 Myles off ye Metinge Hous off Dorchester, Roxberrie, Deadham or Brantree."

From a pecuniary point of view it would seem that the beast hunters held advantage over the office ones. This beastly monopoly, however, was soon broken, and we find in 1653:

"A Bill given to Isaac Bullward off 20s for killyng one Wolve to bee payd bye ye Constple. Also A Bille given toe Thos Herringe off 6s 8d for his Pt in ye Killynge off a Woolfe."

In 1666, Thomas Speene, one of our Indian residents, thus earned a most welcome ten shillings. This was the Indian who, with Waban and John Speene, both redmen, and closely connected with the Rev. John Eliot's Christian Indian settlement, was in 1661 sued by the town in the long controversy over certain lands claimed by both parties.

Among the mighty hunters of those early days were Samuel Hunting, 1670, "the Indean" Cock Robin, who turned in his first wolf in 1674; Eleazer Metcalf and Nathaniel Richards, 1675; Seth Smith, who achieved the same honor in 1676; John Dean; Benj. Miles, three wolves in 1681; Amos Fisher, two shillings three pence for killing nine hawks the same year; Barakiah Lewis, two wolves in 1697; Daniel Draper, two wolves same year; John Draper, one wolf same year; and above all, one Joseph Colburn who thus filled not only his purse with coin, but his chest with convenient corn and peas.

Meantime there were here, also, enforced hunters, hunters of the redskin. In 1675 we find this record:

"A Moshun beinge maid toe ye Towne whither thay woud bare ye Charge of ye Heelyng of John Haws Leage that was hurted in provydinge Timbur for Fortyfycaton referinge toe securynge ye Towne from ye Endians and this was voated in ye Afarmitiv."

As early as 1673 we find the following:

"Upon Sighte of Warante from Athoritie whereas in ye Comitie of ye Militiae air required toe putt ye Souljers in a Postur of Ware, and fyndinge ye Towne defectiv off a stock off Poulder, Bulits and Mach, it is therfor agrede to mak a Rat for ye leving soe much Paye as will procure soe mutch amonifhun as ye Lawe requir. En Dan Fisher Timy Dwite and Tho Fullar ar desird to peur thiss Amonifhun afore sayd."

The next year, this same Thomas Fuller assumes further responsibility, by no means light, as follows:

"1674. Whearas Ser. Thos Fullar was fomerlie deputed to tak Caer off ye Townes Amonifhun it is further agrede with hym that hee shall pvide a convainiant Plas in ye Metinge Hous att ye Townes Chardg to secur ye aforsayd Amonifhun and to dispofe off it att his Diferesfhun; pvided allwaies their bee no Vacantcie off ye Townes Amonifhun, for whitch Care and Truste we doe ingadg to alow him equall sattiffacfhun."

The war cloud came swiftly on, some of the families here slain, and in the very first of 1676 the settlers record:

"Ye Towne bye Voate declar yt noe Persone shall entertayne eny Indine in toe eny Famalie whatsoe ever except Ephrame Endine and yt noe Endine shall reside with in ye Towne Bowndes with oute Aprobashun from ye Select Men toe bee Chofen."

The Indian called Ephraim had for years owned land, paid taxes, and lived peaceably among them, a most useful citizen, but many other redskins, equally peaceable and innocent, were forced to feel the rod.

Two barrels of powder were bought for ten pounds, three hundredweight of lead for bullets for four pounds, and matches for the match-lock guns, then the only firearm in use, twelve shillings six pence. The "greate Gunn" was brought out and remounted and a war tax levied on all within the town. So we find:

> "In Anſer to ye voate of ye Towne wherebye thay have declard thar Onwillingeneſs to have eny Indine entertaynd in ye Towne, ye Select Men doe give Peter Woodard Juner Warninge yt ye firſt Oportunetie, hee doe dispoose off or putt thos Indines that nowe liv with hym oute off this Towne."

This was followed by similar orders to all having Indian house or farm help, then so common, but after this war, superseded by negro slaves of which no less than four were held in Walpole territory alone.

The Indian was not the only unwelcome resident in early times, though for somewhat of a less reason new arrivals were not as now received with open arms.

> "In 1679 Mr Harise and Mr Steevens makinge a Moshun toe Sojorne at Eaſter Fishers Hous for Sum Tyme ye Select Men takinge intoe Conſiderashun and findinge itt not agreeinge with ye Lawe, nor of soe goode Repourte being no Hed of ye Famylie, did not se cauſ to Alow them."

In 1672 we find the following disposition of the young men:

"7 yt ye younge Men bee caled that Cear might bee taken for thair Setelmnt accordyng toe Lawe, Elic Wood is allowed to Sojourne with John Richards, Nat Heaton with Vid Chickring, and John Deen with John Gaye; Jona Metcalfe with his Father Smith; Robt. Alin with Micall Metcalfe and John Fullar Juner with his Farther."

In 1679 we find the following:

"Eenformashun was givn of a Woman whos nam is Smith, an ondesyrabel Pson that nowe liveth at Meadfild and doth intende to builde uppon sum off our Towne Lande, ye Select Men ar defird and empowrd to manage an Odder or doe eny Leagall Acte to pervnt Her or any Pson Coming in such maner without our Libertie from ye Towne."

By this Walpole lost, at least, one early comer which, perhaps, if Dedham had foreseen the future, she would have gladly seen settle down here. So also the widow Pettee, with a young and by no wise small family, was promptly ordered out of town. While some lonely women, like the widows Ellis and Dunkly, who for £3 a year rang the bell on Sundays, kept the meeting-house clean and looked out for the safety of its doors and window-glass, fared pretty well, the majority, on account of poverty alone, had to set their faces squarely away from old Dedham.

One of these widows, good soul, not disturbed, however, always rises before our admiring contemplation for her angelic conduct as described in the following record:

"The town fathers by vote were obliged to assign seats to all in the meeting house. Samuel Gay was dissatisfied with his, but they responded that they saw no cause to change. Mr. Dewing declared his intense displeasure and did not tarry for an agreeable adjustment.

Ralph Freeman would not take his seat because his wife had none. The wife of John Aldus must have her seat up front in the middle row. Richard Everett privately interceeded for his much displeased consort, but Widow Morse, like the peacmaker that she was, kindly came forward and quietly offered to exchange seats with Mrs. Everett, or anyone else dissatisfied with their lot."

After fully contemplating this little discordant church scene, one feels prompted to an instant call for old Joshua Kent, who some time before had been invested with just the powers and duties that the occasion demanded, by the follow ng vote of the town:

"Leift. Fifher is deputed to treate wth Jofhua Kent & Conclude wth him for ye Beateing ye Drume; he is defird to put ye Decons in Minde to put ye Worke yt Jams Allin now do into ye Handes of ye sd Jofhua yt he may Ceareful attende ye Shutringe ye Meteing houfe Doores & ye Kepeing oute ye Doggs & furder we apoynt ye sd Jofhua to bee grave maker for ye Occafons of ye Towne in Genrall and ye Keper of ye Pounde."

CHAPTER III

IN 1674 we find the following reference to the owner of the sawmill here

"Tho Clap mad a Moshun and defird toe keepe his Mayd Servent, — Wee anserd yt wee see noe Reeson toe alowe her butt that hee should remoove her out off ye Towne."

Before the end of the year he prevailed on the town to allow him to keep her and other help on giving the following bond:

"This Wrighting witneffeth yt I Thomas Clape of Deadham doe binde over mye Sawe Mille and alle my Rites and Priviledges there unto belonginge toe ye Select Men off Deadham; and thier fucceffors for ever uppon Condishun yt nether Hen Earle nor Eliz Lenord shall bee eny Trubbel or Damedge bye them or ether of them untoe this Towne Witneffe mye Hande 10 28, 1674.

THOMAS CLAP."

The same year Dedham made the following grant to him here:

"Upon a Moshun of Tho Clap desiringe to exchang a Tracte of Lande contayninge six Akers fomerly graunted to Liu. Fisher deceafed, as itt lyeth neere ye Sawe Mille Parth, on ye Easte Syde off ye Ridge, itt is Upplande and Swampe Meddowe; graunted untoe Tho Clape five Akers adjoyninge uppon one Aker off Lande of ye sayd Clapes or upon his Hom Lott to bee layd oute att ye Defcrefhun of Isaac Bulward and Jams Vales."

In 1663 we find the following reference to another of the first settlers here, Samuel Parker, who lived near the Royal Smith place on Major's Plain:

"Samuel Parker moving for a Peell off Swampie Lande betweene Spice Brooke & ye Lande hee bot off Joshua Fisher."

The old cart path through the Common up to the hill on the south went through this settler's land, but was, at his request, afterwards changed.

In 1664 we find the following reference to this and two other settlers here, showing the inconvenience of living too far from the centre of the town:

"Wheras Samll Parker James Vales and Quinton Stockwell apear bye ye Surveyers toe be behinde in thair Pporſhun of Highe Waye Worke, and thay aledginge thay never had Notis off ye Dayes apointed for yt Worke it is ordered that thay shall yett pforme thar Worke in ye High Waye neere ye Sawe Mille."

Thus as early as 1663 what is now called the centre of Walpole had four settlers: Thomas Clap, James Fales, Samuel Parker, and Quinton Stockwell. Soon after they were joined by Joseph Kingsbury, as appears from the following:

"10 29, 1679. James Vales Seno. Tho Clape Josep Kingsberrie and Jams Vales Juner is toe finysh their Remander off their Worke aboute yt was Quints Hous and ye otther defecktiv Plas adjoyning toe ye Sawe Mille."

The value of their dwelling-houses in 1677 is thus given:

"Jams Vales Senr £5, Jams Vales Juner £2, Tho Clape £2, Sam Parker £2."

In 1667, three of these settlers are referred to in the following order, concerning the use of common lands:

"Jams Vales Sam Parker, Tho Clape ar alowd this Yeare toe cutt ye sam Medowe they had graunted ye laſt Yeare, and toe Jams Vales & Sam Parker Libertie toe cutt Ech off them 3 Lode in ye Est or Sou Est Pt off Toyles Ende Medowe."

It would be pleasant to know how much these isolated settlers contributed in 1668 towards the following:

"Tymo. Dwite is choſn and apoyntd to riceve ye Countrybuſhn yt shall bee brot in from ye Inhabbitanc toward ye Charg off ye Frai: off ye Shippe Lode off Marsts toe bee sente and prſented to His Majties acordyng toe ye Ordere off ye Generall Corte. A bil is ordyrd to bee givn toe Mr Man ye Skoole Marſter toe receave Tenn Pnds off ye Cunstapel in Fulle off his Sallerie for ye last Yere."

In 1669 appears a new comer here:

"Left Fisher give Notis to ye Selecte Men yt Caleb Church is placed as tenant att ye Sawe Mille."

The same year Dedham made this additional grant:

"Graunted toe Samll Parker 8 or 10 Akrs off Lande lyeing neere ye Sawe Mille on ye North Syde off ye Waye leedinge to ye Pyn Swampe and ajoyneing ye Weste Syd off ye Brooke caled Spice brooke, toe bee layed oute bye ye Defereſſhun and Estimashun of Nath Coalburn and Tymo Dwite."

This pine swamp lay just east of the brook now called Spring Brook, and became later the site of the sawmill of Deacon Fales.

In 1672 we find reference to two additions to the little colony here, Caleb Church and the following:

"This Daye Isak Bulward psent a Moshun for Libertie toe Leat his Hous & Lande that was somtyme Quintin Stokewels toe a yonge mann."

"Graunted unto Caleb Church aboute halfe an aker off upplande his Hous standing uppon itt."

The preceding year the town had ordered Caleb Church to give the following bond:

"Knoe alle Men bye thees Prefnts yt I Caleb Church of Deadham liveinge neere ye Sawe Mille doe ingag myself my Heyers and Eftat toe ye Select Men off Deadham and thayer Succeffers in ye Behalfe off ye Towne to safe ye sayd Towne off Deadham free from alle Charge and Trubbel from or bye Fraunces Joanes nowe Refidnt with mee, or for wante thereoff to paie too ye sayd Select Men or thayer Succeffers for ye Ufe off ye sayd Towne ye fule and Juste som off Thirtie Powndes in god Countrey paiemt, toe bee well and trulye mad and dun I binde mifelf my Heyers, Exectrs and Admnftratrs firmelie by thefe Prsnts — Wittnes mye Hande heere untoe fubfcribd 10, 19 1671.

CALEB CHURCH."

In 1692, this part of Dedham gained another permanent addition in William Robins, as the name was first spelled, who settled near the church land of the town on both sides of the Neponset River, a close neighbor of Peter Fales, Sr. Two years later came Joseph Hartshorn and settled down just below the falls of the river but near both Fales and Robins on one side of the old Sawmill road, and Thomas, Eleazer, and Thomas Clapp on the other, and at the first town meeting after the arrival of Hartshorn the following reference is made:

"Jofep HartfHorne and Willm Roobins doe both move toe ye Prpriatrs toe graunte toe them Timbur off thayr comon Lande toe fenc & bild uppon thayr Lande wch thay bot in ye Towne neereunto ye Sawe Mille. Ye Prpreters graunted thayer Ption toe them."

A few months later the town passed the following measure, of so little benefit to settlers way up here:

"It being then pposed to ye Towne whither ye one halfe Pte off ye Sallary for ye Mayntaynanc off ye Schole shall bee levyed uppon ye Pairents or Marster off Suche Mal Childrn af live within three Mile off ye Meteyng Hous, or therabouts, off ye adg off Seaven Yeres & under Twelv Yeeres olld for this prsent Affefmnt. This was voated in ye Affermatif. It beinge further prpofd to ye Towne whithar ye othere Half Pte off ye above menshund Sallery shall bee levyd uppon Esteats onily and noe Pte off itt upon Heds, this allsoe was voated in ye afyrmativ."

During this same year appears a reference to one who for years hired and pastured Dorchester's 300 acre old School Farm, then forming a portion of East Walpole territory, and who kept a public house on the old Post road, at which the first stage stopped after crossing King's bridge at the Neponset just below.

"Upon ye Requeste off Henrey White, ye Towne have grаunted him Libertie toe ereck & Sett up a Smale Hous neere ye Meteinge Hous for his Convenance upon ye Sabath. And have leftt itt toe ye Select Men toe apoynt ye Plas toe Sett upp ye sayd Hous in."

In 1698 William Robbins petitioned for a bound between him and the church land:

"Upon ye Moshun off William Robins yt ye Lyne betwene ye Church Lott and him att ye Sawe Mille mite bee rune, John Deene is deputed thereunto with Wm. Avery."

And again the same year, as follows:

"Willm Robins off ye Sawe Mille did this Daye move toe ye Ppieters toe send Men toe runn ye Lyne betwene his Lott purcheffd off Thos.

Clap and ye Comon Lande ye Prprieters bye voate declar thay leve ye Car off yt Conceerne with ye Select Men."

In 1705, at the March meeting, Dedham took action about her Common and waste land up here, which included a large part of what is now the centre of Walpole and, for years, called the Sawmill Dividends.

"Itt was putt toe ye Voate off ye Prprieters whither thay wille Laye oute in Devident all thair undevided Landes lyeinge on ye Southerlie Syde off Joseph Heartshornes on bothe Sydes off Naponset Rivere, this was answeard in ye afermatif. This Daye abov sayd ye Pprieters haveing Concluded toe Laye oute in Devident alle thayr Comon or undevideed Lande lyinge on ye Southerlie Syde off Josep Hartshornes on bothe Sydes off Naponsett Riviere, itt was further putt toe ye Voate off ye Ppropriaters and ye Commity whither ye Sirvayer and ye Commity apoyntid and Chosen toe Laye oute sd Divident shalle take a Circumfranc thareoff and diserib itt and ye Pprieters drawe thair Lottes for itt ethyr bye fiftie Akers or one hundred Akers in a Lott which of them thay shall fynd most equall and convenyant, this was ansurd in ye Afermatif."

This was followed by what ever after were called the Sawmill dividends, above referred to, and the following question which soon became the chief cause of our separation from the mother town:

"On ye 4th daye of March 1706 aforsayd severall off ye Inhabertanc off this Towne which atende Publik Worshipe in othyr Townes and haf payd in thayr Pproposhuns toe ye Sallery in Pte or in Wholl at suche Plases and hav neglektid toe atend ye Towne Ordere tharin bye bringeing in a Certiferkat tharoff in seeson, did this Daye aply themselvs toe ye Towne and make Requeste that thay mite bee relefed off soe mutch off thayr Pproshun toe sayd Sallery as thay did presente a Cirtiffikat that thay hav payd att othere Plases for ye Year 1704."

"Ye Towne did thareuppon graunte thair Requeaste and Josep Hartshorne in perticuler was relesed allthoug hee hade nott payd his whol Pprofshun, upon Considerashun that hee had been ovrchargd in an Assesmente, this abov writtn refere to ye yere 1704 onely."

In 1679, while the Rev. William Adams was pastor, the town in its March meeting ordered:

"That thos Men belongeing toe ye Sawe Mille, with Isak Chinery, are toe paye toe ye Revernd Mr John Willson two third Ptes off thair Rats and toe bringe his Recaite which shall bee thayr Discharg for soe mutch in or as Mony and ye other third Pte toe Mr Will Adams Pastour."

Mr. Wilson was the minister at Medfield.

While they were wrestling with the church attendance question, another of far greater importance arose:

"In 11, 30 1683. This Daye after Lectur itt was putt toe Voate off ye Fremen and Inhabitanc whither thay did desyre that Govr and Companie woulde defende thar Charter and Privilidgs soe farr as thay can, this was (soe farr as coulde bee desarnd) unniversially voated in ye Afermitif. Itt beinge putt toe tham iff thay ar willinge wee shoud make a full Submisshun and eintyr Resignashun toe his Majestyes Pleshur as in his Deklarashun is intimated, itt was all voated in ye negetiv."

This is preceded by an item not quite so clear or agreeable to consider:

"A Bil is given toe Sergt Wm Averey toe receve 5s off ye Constabel in ful Sattifaxun for Emplay stringe uppon ye Corps off our lat Revend Pastur, this is toe bee payd out off ye Assesmt for Monie toe difra ye Chargs off Our Pasters Funerall."

Alas, what was it the sergeant did! Was it something so special that its proper execution demanded a warrior bold? It must have covered the gallant "Trayning Bande" with everlasting glory. Preceding such strong resolutions to be a free people it may have been intended to warn all enemies, and especially the king, of the terrible fate surely awaiting them.

In 1678 appears a reference to another early settler in what was once Walpole but afterward South Dedham territory:

"Ezra Mors make a Moshun toe hav Libertie to flud a smalle Peell off Lande refereinge toe a Sawe Mille uppon ye Broke cald Ed Hawses in ye Waye ledinge to Foule Medowe."

This Dedham settler had several years before gained the franchise for a grist-mill above that of Nathaniel Whiting on Mother or Mill Brook, but was beset by so many trials from both this old business rival and fellow-townsmen he yielded to the demands of the town to lower his pond, and allowed his dam to be taken down and moved south towards our sawmill, across what is often called Ellis Pond and brook, which, at that early period, had been called after Dedham's first mason and painter, Ed. Hawes, Hawes's Brook.

Either he or his son Ezra, Jr., settled on what is now Mylod Street; this street, having been obtained by him, and for years called after him, Lieut. Morse's Road.

The northern boundary of Walpole for many years was this brook, and this man's family, one of the more prominent in town, furnished one of our first selectmen and our second town clerk, while his dwelling became one of our first schoolhouses. Dedham granted him, in consideration of his giving up his Mill-brook rights, the following:

"March 18, 1670 Upon a Moshun mad by Ezra Mors ye Pprieters Chofe and deputed Samll Gaye Jonn Metcaff & John Deane a Comity toe laye oute toe Ezra Mors yt fortie Akers off Lande graunted toe him for his Incuredgemente toe lett fale his corne Mille for ye leting downe off ye Watter for ye Benifit off our Medows & ye othere Milles. Feb. 2, 1698 Ezra Mors makeinge Demaunds off Sattiffacshun for ye Ufe off his Hous ye laste Yere toe Keepe ye skule in ye Select Men agreed with him yt hee should receeve off ye Towne fiveteen Shillinge in ful Sattiffaxion upon yt Accounte."

The school requirements of that period were:

"That thofe Inhabitanc yt dwel mor then twoe Mils and A Haf from ye Schule shall bee frede from al Charge off Rats uppon their Childrenes Heds for ye Schole until thay shall receve Benifit therbye and then shall bee rated and paye as thofe within A Mil and a Quarter allwayes pvided yt such Childrin bee taken Car off so as thay bee Sufichunt toe rede and wrighte."

The following arrangement was made for the proposed division of the Sawmill lands, mentioned above as including the greater part of what was afterward the centre of Walpole:

"This 17th of May 1708, aforefaid the propriators being met upon due Notis given & upon trial, it did appear that the Majourity of Propriators were prefent to act. The faid propriators of this Town of Dedham taking into their Confideration how to finifh the Laying out of that Devident of Land agreed upon to be Layed out on the Southerly fide of Jofeph Hartfhorns, Doe agree & by their Votes doe declare their mind is Notwithftandin all former Vote in that Cafe that every perticular Propriator shall have Liberty to draw a Lot of his perticuler proprotion in faid Devidents. It was allso put to the Vote of the propriators whither ſo many of the propriators ſhall agree to draw their lots together in any lot may have the Liberty, and this was Anſwered in the Afermitive.

"It likwis alſo was put to the Vote of the propriators whither they will have four Acres to one cow common right layd out in ſayd Devident This was likewis anſwered in the Affermitive. It was further Voted that everyone of the propriators as ſhall ſee Cauſe to Draw their Lots at preſent in ſaid Devident Doe bring in their Names to the Town clerk with the Number of their Common rights on Munday the twenty-fourth of this Inſtant May by three of the Clock in the after noon and then to make so many lots as there Doth appear rights of the propriators to draw — and ſaid lots being Drawn ſhall be layd out ſucceſſively according to Number of Each lot, the firſt lot begi.nning next to Mr. Pages farme according as the ſervayers and Commity which have taken the ſircumferanse of ſaid Devident have deſcribed it and given it in in Writting this 17th of May aforeſaid. This likwis was anſwered in the Afermitive. The ſaid diſcription as it was given in Writting by the Commity & ſirvayed 17 of May aforeſaid is as followeth.

"We thinck it is the Conveninteſt to begin the firſt lot where Mr Pages farme doth end, to head on Dorcheſter Line upon the Square, and to Continue till Dorchiſter line and Wrentham line doth meet, and on Naponcet River Propriaty and Seder Swamp. And the next Deviſion to begin at the Corner of the Great Seder Swamp near the great ſhaving place & to head upon ſaid Swamp and Naponcet River except where propirators cuts them off, and ſo to end next to William Robinses. The next to begin where the Devident called Medfield Devident abuts on Medfield line and to abutt upon ſaid Devident and Stop River except when propriators doth cut them ofe, and ſo to Continue as one Devident Begining where the Wrentham line doth meet with Claps Meadow; and ſo abutting upon ſaid line Square and the Seder Swamp and Medfield Devident ſo far as land may be prophitable to be layed out to the propriators.

"May 24 the propriators being met to draw their lots and they not being finiſhed before night did appoynt to meet againe the next training day.

"June 14. The propirators being met after training ſuch as did appear which had not drawn their lots drue them. It was this day put to the vote of the proprieters whither they will Impower John Deane, their fervayer in laying out these Lots in this Devident of land next above mentioned. This was anfwered in the Afirmative. It was likewis put to the vote of the propriators whither they do Choos Capt. Daniell fifher one of a commity to Joyne with the faid furvayers in laying out the lots in faid Devident this was anfwered in the Afirmative.

"It was alfo put to the vote of the propriators wither they doe choos Capt Samuell Guild one of faid Commity. This was anfwered in the Afirmitive. Itt was put to the propriators whither the propriators of the Farme called pages farme fhall have notis given them to run the line between said farme and the wast land of the propriators of the Town of Dedham. This was anfwered in the Afirmative. It was further put to the vote of the said propriators aforesaid whether they doe apoynt & Deput Capt Daniell Fifher & Capt Samuel Guild and John Deane their agents to act in the behalfe of said propriators of Dedham in runing faid line. This was anfwered in the Afirmative.

"Upon the motion made by Ebenezer fales to have his land in this Devident layed out Joyning to his land neer home informed the three men soe above named to lay out said land to Ebenezer fales. On the mofion made by Amos fifher & Joseph Hartshorn to have their land in faid Devident Joyning to their own land. This was answered in the Afirmative."

William Robins was constable in 1708, perhaps our first representative in that important office. Then follows a reference to one of the old roads:

"In April 1708 Affembled Nathaniel Gay, John Smith, Timothy Whitting & William Avery.

"Allfoe in anfwer to a motion made by Leit Jofeph Colburn and others of their neighbors to have a way layed out from the road leading to Medfield neer their houfes to the Country Road neer the houfe of Leit Barakiah Lewifes; said Selectmen doe defir and Appoynt said Commity (Capt Samuel Guild, Joseph Fairbanks and Samuel Whiting) to take a view of the Neceffity and Convenience thereof & the proposed said way that it may be obtained with as littel damag to any in their propriaty as may be and make reporte thereof to the Towne or Select-men their first oportunity."

Following is an item of the payment of "19 shillings to Leiut Barakiah Lewis, for work on the cart Bridge," and the following:

"Oct. 14, 1712. Affembled Capt Samuell Guild, Serg John Ellice & Jofeph Wright. This day the Selectmen have given order for the constables to warn such persons as have not drawn their lots in the Devident of land on the southerly side of Jofeph Hartshorns to appear at the Meting houfe on the twentyth day of Inftant October at four of the clock in the afternoon after Trayning To give in the number of their Commons and to draw their lots in faid devident.

"Oct the 20, 1712 this day the Selectmen being met at the Meting houfe after Trayning. Severall perfons Appear to draw their lots in that Devident of land on the Southerly side of Jofeph Hartshorns, Namely, Capt Daniel Fifher to draw upon the Rights which he had purchafed of Left James Fifher and Andrew Dewing. Alfo Sergt Benjamin Onion to draw upon the Rights he had bought up which were Edward Cooks and Nathaniel Bullards. Also Ebenezer Fales to draw upon the Rights he had of Daniel Wight and Jofeph Dammon and Eleazer Clape, thefe did on faid day give in the Numbers of their Commons and drew their Lots in said Devident."

In 1713 the term moderator first appears. In 1714 Joshua Clap was chosen constable, but petitioned to be allowed a substitute, and Joseph Hartshorn surveyor:

"Feb the 7th, 1714 Affembled Capt Samuel Guild Sergt Timothy Whiting, Jofeph Ellice, Michael Metcalf & Jofeph Wight at the houfe of Jofhua Fifher and Severall perfons there aperd to draw their lots in the Devident of land called the Sawmill devident, as Lieft John Baker to draw for part of the Rights that were Mr Daniel Allins & John Deane Sen. to draw for part of the Rights that were Lieft John Bakers, and John Richards to draw for the Rights which were John Fullers, Sen., thefe perfons this 7th Daye of Febr. did give in the number of their Commons and draw their Lots in sd Devident."

Ebenezer Fales was chosen constable in 1714–15, thus indicating increasing influence of this part of Dedham.

In June, 1715, we find the following reference to the Plain road:

"Upon the defire of several perfons to have a highway laid out by the houfe of Thomas claps to Stop river, the Selectmen have deputed Sergt John Ellice, William Bullard and John Metcalf a Committee to view and lay out sd way where it may be most convenent for the Towns ufe, and leaft damage to any person two rods wide."

Under June 5, 1715, appears this reference to the second keeper of "Stronge Watters" in town:

"This day alfo the Selectmen have given their approbation that John Richards may receive a Litence to keep an Houfe of publick entertainment in Dedham."

On the determination of the town of Dedham to draw lots for the large tract of land lying between Paige's Farm on the east, land of Joseph Hartshorn and the Neponset River on the north, and the Dorchester, Wrentham and Dedham lines, new life was infused into this part of the town.

In 1685 the last legal Indian claim had been extinguished by the purchase of the triangular tract of two hundred acres, at the junction of the Neponset River and the easterly town line, by Nathaniel Paige, of Boston. At that period all the Walpole territory on the east and south of the Neponset, south from Lewis Lane in East Walpole to South Walpole, lay common, of no use to any one, and was known as waste land. This, after a more or less careful survey, according to the above vote in general town meeting, was declared open to all freemen of Dedham.

These lots, or dividends as they were then termed, on account of being divisions out of land in which all had an equal right, for the most part were long and narrow, of varied length, and ran pretty much northwest by southeast from river, or in a few cases settled farms, to the different town lines.

The First Sawmill Dividend was small and irregular and at what was, some seventy-five years later, the Stanley-Maxey and afterwards the Daniel Ellis mill property, since purchased by the Plimpton family, in whose hands it remains to-day.

The Second Sawmill Dividend fell by lot to Thomas Paine and comprised twelve acres. This now forms a part of the easterly boundary of the present Lewis Farm, and the westerly boundary of the old Isaac Lewis Farm and Lane.

The Third Dividend contained twenty-eight acres and fell in 1712 to Thomas Metcalf. Soon after Walpole was set off from Dedham, a house and barn was erected on this lot by either Timothy Foster or Joseph Coney, subsequent owners. This was purchased just after the close of the French and Indian war by one of that war's veterans, John Lewis, whose father, Isaac Lewis, had

THE FIRST HOUSE ON THE THIRD SAWMILL DIVIDEND (THE JOHN LEWIS DAVID LEWIS PLACE, EAST STREET)

For a few years in the prior possession of Timothy Foster and Joseph Coney

THE FIRST BUILDING ON THE FOURTH SAWMILL DIVIDEND

With the exception of some twenty years of the early part of the eighteenth century the sole individual possession of the Isaac Lewis family

some twenty-five years before purchased over sixty acres adjoining on the south. The Fourth Dividend of more than sixty acres, and the first lot to extend across from river to Dorchester line, fell in 1715 to Sergt. Eleazer Kingsbury; to be more explicit, to his heir Jeremiah Dexter, a blomor, who soon sold to Isaac Lewis, who, at the time Walpole became a town, owned what was afterwards known as the John Fairbanks place, in what is now East Walpole, his widow afterwards marrying the latter. Of this early settler, the Fairbanks family history contains a brief but glowing tribute. The deed by which he received this Fourth Dividend contains as witnesses the names of the first permanent minister of our town and of his first wife, Phillips and Anne Payson.

The Fifth Dividend was taken in 1719 by several inhabitants, Comfort Starr, 20¾ acres; Ephraim Wilson, Jr., 16 acres; Jabez and William Pond, 12 acres, 16 rods; Nath Gay, 4 acres; Lusher Gay, 12 acres.

The Sixth Dividend, Samuel Gay Sr., 16 acres; John and Timothy Gay, 16 acres each.

The Seventh Dividend, 64 acres, Joseph and Joseph Wight, Jr.; Capt. Daniel Fisher, Jeremiah and Daniel Fisher, Jr., 52 acres.

The Eighth Dividend in 1721, to Ensign Robert Avery, 28 acres; Capt. John Baker, 44 acres; Samuel Gay.

The Ninth Dividend, Capt. Samuel Guild, 58 acres.

The Tenth Dividend, heirs of William Avery, 32 acres; heirs of Jonathan Avery, 28 acres.

The Eleventh Dividend, Samuel Bullard, Ezra Morse, Peter and Samuel Thorp.

The Twelfth Dividend, Dea. Jonathan Metcalf and James Fales.

Thus they continued, with a right of way through reserved from the first to the last, which from the first to the eleventh soon became the only way from what is now East Walpole to the Old Sawmill Road which, until eight years after this town was set off from the mother town, was merely a rough cart path fit only for ox-teams; the present East Street way through the Sand-hill over the railroad bridge having, many years after, been hurriedly built at night, to escape an injunction from the courts. From the Allen and Fales neighborhood, the reserved way wound around anywhere through what is now the land of Melzar W. Allen by the Diamond Pond, passing through Spice or Spring Brook up the hill, and then taking a short cut through Major's Plain up and over the hill to the old Sawmill and the Dorchester line.

After the town could satisfy the conditions of their incorporation by settling a minister and providing for a meeting-house and school, they at once turned their tardy attention to the improvement of its roads. But it was not until 1727, three years after we became a town, that the first earnest effort was made. This was as follows:

"May ye 24, 1727. Affembled ye Selectmen and appoynted John Guilde Survayer to mend ye High Wayes on ye Northeasterly syde of ye Brook between Ebenezer Fales & Tho Claps with ye Hands on ye same syde of ye Brook excepting Robert Allen, and apoynted Ebenezer Robins to mend ye Highwaye on ye South westerly syde of ye Brook, with ye Hands on ye same till we come to Chamberlins Frame, and that

Robert Allen work under him, and apoynt Eleazer Partridge to mend ye Highways from there to Stop river."

The "Brook" was Spice or Spring brook, and the "Frame" or farm near the Horace Guild place on what was called Easy Plain.

In 1715 for the first time appear the Walpole names of Timothy Morse, Ebenezer Turner, Samuel Kingsbury, John Boyden, all old Walpole Plain settlers, and Bernam Farrington, an old neighbor of Ezra Morse in the east part of the town.

In 1716 Peter Fales, Sr., who lived just north of Spice brook, was chosen surveyor.

In September, 1717, the following appears concerning a change in the main street in the Centre:

"In Anfwer to a Motion made by severall of the Inhabitants of this Towne liveing near the old saw mill to have the way by the houfe of Thomas Clap altered to the right-hand through the land of William Robbins Sen. where there is a bridg and a way in use already, and to go on till it meet with the old highway again, the town has chofen Jofeph Hartshorn, Sen, John Everit and Daniel Draper a committie to lay out sd way."

This change located Main Street where it now crosses Spring Brook.

Unlike this part of old Dedham most of the well-known streets in Dedham Centre were already laid out. In addition to those already mentioned, several were built under the following vote:

"July 17th 1700. Afsembled after lectur Capt. Daniell Fifher Leut. Samuel Guild, Sergt Josiah Fifher & Wm Avery. This day the Selectmen Chofe and Deputid Deacon Thomas Metcalfe and (Lieut)

Barakiah Lewis a commity to lay out neccessery High Ways from the Old Sawe Mille Road to the Fields at Naponfeet River So as may be moft Convenent & leaft prejudifhall for ye Town and perticuler Perfones."

This was seventeen years before this part of the town had a bridge at either of the river crossings near the Common. The old way was to make a fording place, which always served for a watering place as well. It is but a few years since such a one was removed in front of the store of Hartshorn Brothers. This was a part of the old powder house lot which extended to beyond the present freight house of the old New York and New England railroad, and had been from earliest times a most convenient and useful watering place.

In early times, however, the settlers here were more anxious to save their strength than to procure unnecessary watering places for their animals. They dreaded and tried to avoid going the long distance to church and town meeting. Petition after petition was sent in, and under May the 16, 1717, appears a vote granting the following privilege:

"It was furder proposed if it be the mind of the Town that the Estat of the persons at the old saw mill, and other perfons estat liveing five miles from the Meting houfe, shall be afsefed to the Minifters Salary, freeing them of their head money provided they pay their head money to the place where they constantly hear and bring under the hand of ye receiver that they have so done. Voted in the Afirmative."

In January, 1717–18, it was voted that the school, which had always been in the centre of the town, should be "removed to several parts of this town."

The same year appears, as petitioned above, the straightening of the main street here:

"Sept 17, 1717. Wee whofe names are hereunto fubfcribed haveing received an order to lay out a way between the houfe of Wiliam Robbin Sen, and the road to the ceder swamp, wee have laid out sd way as followeth viz wee have left the old road in peter woodwards lot, the way is laid out two rods wide through the land of peter falls, sen. and the land of William Robbins sen as wee have marked it out along by the weft side of the land of Ebenezer falls and so thro the land of Wiliam Robbins sen. two rods wide till it comes to wrentham Road. Jofeph Hartshorn, Daniel Draper John Everit."

This is followed by the following graphic statement of public duty, 1718:

"This 16th day of April the felectmen have agreed with Jarvis Pike to sweep the meeting houfe, and ring the bell on Sabbath days and on publick days, and at nine of the clock in the nighte and alfo to take care of the pound as pound keeper for the prefent. On May 13, 1718 This day also it was put to the town whether they will give leave to Ezra Morfe and his famaly and Barned farington to doe their parte of their high way work for this year at the bridg over the river near or leading to his houfe."

Under July 17, 1718, there was a general town cleaning

"This day the Selectmen have given order for the constable to warn the severall perfons under named to depart out of this town for the Selectmen doe not allow them to continue in this town as Inhabitants. Richard Beten, Robert Worflie, Samuel Edmons, Isaac Bolfter, Thomas Shepifon, Samuel Road, Benj Force, William Owen, and the widow Trot, and her son."

Under May 12, 1719, they turned their attention to other pests not so easily handled:

"This day it was also propofed to the town if it be their mind to allow sixpence for every rattlefnake that any perfon shall kill in this town, and bringing an inch and an half of the end of the tail with the rattle to the town treafurer. Anfwerd in ye Afirmative."

In 1721 appear the names of Eben Hartshorn, Moses Chamberlain, Jeremiah Clark, John Hall, Jeremiah Day, William and Nathaniel Pond, Samuel Shears, Eleazer Partridge, Joseph Smith, Samuel and Ebenezer Ware, and Benjamin Gay. At this time £3 was all the town allowed its representative to General Court, and even at that price was often fined for not furnishing one. Under Nov. 4, 1719, occurs the following:

"This day of November Leiut Jofhua Fifher did Inform the Selectmen that the executor of Mr John Eliot demand mony of this Town for sd Eliots keeping the school in this town long since. The Selectmen have agreed with sd Leiut Fifher to pay the sd debt and to giv a difcharg for the Town, for which the Selectmen have engaged to him three pound in mony in behalf of the town."

This bill, from some unknown reason, had been neglected for years. It may be that the long controversy over the lands claimed from the town for the "pore endines" made it rather hard for the voters to settle any claim bearing the name of this persistent "Apostle."

After bearing their inconveniences in attendance on public worship as long as nature allowed, the settlers here petitioned for the privilege allowed some years before to those of the north part of Dedham. The following was all the reception it received:

"March the 7, 1721. This day the Inhabitants of this town living at or near the old saw mill did prefent their petition to the town desirein the town to free them from payeing to the minifter in this town, in order to have preaching amongst themfelves. Voted in the Negative."

This only aroused the petitioners to try to secure a more free and desirable condition still.

"1721. This 15 day of May severall of the Inhabitants, of the Southerly part of this Town did prfent a petition to the Town defireing the Town to set them off from the Northerly part of the Town in order to be a Townfhip among them. Non Concurred."

One can imagine the feelings that accompanied those repulsed old farmers over the eight miles of their homeward journey that May afternoon, and for many a long day afterward they abated not. Perhaps they looked upon the following misfortune of their too ready opponents as a just retribution:

"Feb 22, 1721. This day the Selectmen have agreed & think it is beft for the Congregation to Meet at the houfe of Jeremiah Halle, the next Sabbath day becaufe many perfons are afraid to goe to the Meeting houfe by reafon of the Infecttion of the small pox."

The records fail to state whether or not there was a general and emphatic non-concurrence to that. Self-interest, probably, guided them in this case as in the other.

There is no record also of Dedham's action on the following:

"March the 6th 1722. This day some of the Inhabitants weftwadly part of this towne did prefent a petition to the town defiringe ye town to set them off as a townfhip or precinct — this day also the Inhabitant of the Clavebordtrees and other Inhabitants of this town did prefent a petition to the town defireing to have the meeting houfe removed, or to be set off as a townfhip or precinct."

Again the settlers here valiantly returned to the charge.

"May 14, 1722. This day the Inhabitants of the South part of this town, at or near the old saw mill, prefented a petition to the Town defireing to be sett off from this town as a townfhip or a precinct. It was propofed to the town if it be their mind to free from paying to the miniftrey, here for the prefent such Inhabitants as live from the town beyond Hawes Brook, and shall agree and doe their part with such of the mentioned Inhabitants to obtain and maintain preaching among themselves. Voted in the Affirmative. It was furder propofed toe the town to choofe a comity to confider the petition of some of the Inhabitants for a townfhip or precinct at or near the old saw mill and to view where may be the most proper place for bounds if they Judg it neceffary & to make Report of the whole to the town at their next generall meeting. Voted in the affirmative."

Following the above comes what must be a reference to Walpole Plain territory, though under a name long forgotten:

"Affembled May the 16, 1722. Capt Samuel Guild, Capt William Avery Lieut John Metcalfe, Lieut Ebenezer Woodward & Jofeph Wight. Upon the petition of Sundrey of the Inhabitants belonging to Eafey plain to have a highWay laid out from Thomas Clapes by their houfes and so to Stop river, and the Selectmen have deputed Capt Jeremiah Fisher, Lieut John Metcalfe and Lieut Ebenezer Woodward to view the sd Way and lay out the same if they think fit."

This year first appear the names of John Guild, Robert Allen, Isaac Lewis, Samuel Petty, taxed for the minister's support.

On the 14th of October, 1723, a call was given to the

Rev. Samuel Dexter to which Ebenezer Fales, one of our most prominent citizens, assented. Mr. Dexter replied as follows:

"Honoured & Beloved

Seeing that the Soverign Jehovah in whose hands are the hearts of all men hath so far united ye afection of the Church and Congregation in this place that they have elected me who am les then ye Least of all saints to the Work of the Evangelicall minestry among you & hath inclined your hearts freely to ofer of your temporall good things so far as you have done for my suport, I doe therefore hereby Declare (though with trembling doe I ingag in so great a Work for who is suficient for the sd things) that I freely embrace your Invitation because I believe it to be my incumbant Duty, and I thanckfuly axcept your ofers & will Relying upon your Generosity, that as you have done so far, you will further be Spirited to doe as my Circumstances may Require. And now humbly hopeing in and Relying upon the Gracious head of influences who Liberaly bestoweth the Gifts and Graces of his holy Spirit to furnish and qualifye me for the Work of the Minestry. Let us strive together in prayer to god that he would make me Skilfull faithfull and Suckcesfull that we may be Crowns of Joy to Each other in the day of Christs Apareing. That God would multiply Grace Mercy and peace to his people in this place, is the Earnest prayer of him who wold Rejoyce to Spend and be spent in the Service of your Souls.

"Samuel Dexter.

"Malden December 6, 1723."

The next reference to any old Walpole settler is to the one generally called Dr. Jero in the early records of Walpole:

"March 3, 1724. This day allso it was proposed to the propriators wether they will grant Doctter Gerorld six acres of land on the southerly side of the Rhoad Leading to Medfield neer the hous of Nathaniel Bullard, to be laid out by the towns Comity. Voted in the Afirmative."

After the long struggle for independence by the settlers here, we find the following:

"May 15, 1724. It was allso put to the town whether it be their mind to Grant the Petition of Severall of the Inhabitants at or neer the old sawe mille that they might have a townſhip. Voted in ye affirmative. Theſe four last votes were decented againſt by Joſeph Ellis, Daniell Draper, John Bacon, John Dean, Ebenezer Dean, John Richards, Luther Gay, Ralph Day, Jeremey Day, John Gay."

And old Jarvice Pike still kept on ringing the bell and sweeping out the dust, dogs, and boys from that old discarded meeting-house as unconcernedly as before, while the old Dedham records make but a most brief reference to her new-born child, and then only as "Wallpole this day set off."

In 1726 Dedham warned our old worthy citizen of the east part of the town, Jeremiah Gould, and his entire family, who had lived there eleven months, out of the town. Josiah Plimpton as peremptorily followed.

CHAPTER IV

THE Petition to the General Court of the seven men from this part of Dedham for a new township is not to be found. It is known that Joshua Clap and William Robbins were two of the number, and tradition adds that Ebenezer Fales, Thomas Clap, Peter Fales, Sr., Joseph Hartshorn, and Ezra Morse were the remainder. However, early in 1724, having at last obtained the consent of the rest of Dedham, a petition was sent in.

Thomas Palmer, a member of the Brattle Street Church in Boston, and member of the Government of the Province of Massachusetts Bay, from the first appeared most friendly towards the measure. The record at the State House runs thus:

"JOURNAL MASSACHUSETTS BAY HOUSE OF REPRESENTATIVES. —

"Martis Die 2, June 10 1724. A Petition of several of the Inhabitants of the Town of Dedham near the Old Saw Mill signed by Wm. Robbins, Joshua Clapp and 5 others in behalf of themselves and the rest of the Petitioners, showing that they have for a long Time labored under great inconvenience by reason of their great Distance from their Public Worship; that they preferred a Petition to the Town of Dedham to set them off for a Township, the said Town well considering their Case at their Meeting held the 15th of May last, were pleased, so far as concerned them, to grant their Petition that they might have a Township or distinct Precinct, that the bounds thereof should extend from Wrentham Bounds to the easterly side of John Everitt's House, and from Dorchester Line straight to Medfield Road fifty Rods Westerly from the Place where Hawes's Brook (so called) crosses Medfield Road, and so on Medfield Road to Medfield Line, Praying that this Court would please to Declare and Constitute them a Township by such Name as to them shall seem meet, And all the Lands comprehended within the said Bounds may be set off in said Township, that they may enjoy all the Privileges and Immunities which other new Towns in the Province by Law have and enjoy.

"Referred to a Committee for which Col. Chandler reported June 12, 1724, in favor of a Committee of suitable persons to be appointed by the Court to repair to Dedham to view the Lands and report at the next session. Speaker Col. Spurr and Mayor Quincey to furnish the Committee."

Committee were Col. Robert Spurr, Representative from Dorchester, Major John Quincey of Braintree, and Col. John Palmer of Woodstock, who visited the territory, the most celebrated party, at that time, to have been upon our streets. The old Buck Tavern close by East Walpole on the old post road, and the Ball near the old sawmill, if they were then in existence, probably both gave them free entertainment. On their return to Court they made their report. Then the record proceeds:

"3d December 1724. Thomas Palmer brought down the Petition of Sundry of the Inhabitants of the Town of Dedham near the old saw mill with the vote or Report of the Committee of both Houses thereon as Entered in last Courant, pas'd in Council viz. December 2nd 1724. Read and non-concurred, and the Board insist on their former Vote. Sent down for concurrence. Read and nonconcurred, and House insist on their vote.

"Dec. 7 1724. An Act for Dividing up the Town of Dedham by

Erecting a new Town under the name of Walpole. Read a second and third day and passed to be Enacted."

This is the first mention of the intended name of the new town upon the records. There was some difference of opinion as to what the new town should be called, thus causing delay, but as Sir Robert Walpole had for three years past been prime minister of England and her Colonies, and had always proved their true and ever helpful friend, this little struggling community gladly accepted the honor of his name. The record thus goes on:

"Thomas Palmer Esq of Boston brought down the full vote of Council in council Dec. 10, 1724. Ordered that Mr. Ebenezer Fa es, a principal Inhabitant of the Town of Walpole, be and hereby is directed and impowered to Notify and Summon the Inhabitants duly Qualified for Voting, to assemble and to meet together for Choosing of Town Officers to stand unto the next Annual Election according to Law. Read and concurred."

The Act incorporating Walpole stands thus:

"ACTS AND LAWS

Paffed by the Great and General Court or Affembly of His Majefty's Province of the Maffachufetts Bay in New England Begun & Held at Bofton upon Wednefday the Twenty-feventh of May 1724. And continued by feveral Prerogations Unto Wednefday the Eleventh Day of November following and then Met.

"An Act for the Dividing the Town of Dedham and making a new Town there by the name of Walpole.

"Preamble: WHEREAS the South Part of the Town of Dedham within the County of Suffolk is compresetly settled with Inhabitants who labor under great difficulties by their Remoteness from the Place of Public

Worship &c, and have thereon made their Application to the said Town of Dedham, and likewise addressed this Court, that they be set off a distinct and separate Town and be Vested with all the Powers and Privileges of a Town, And the Inhabitants of Dedham having Consented to their being set off accordingly, and a Committee of this Court having Viewed the said Town of Dedham and Reported a proper Divisional Line between the Two Parts thereof. Be it therefore Resolved by the Lieutenant Governor, Council and Representatives in General Court Assembled and by the Authority of the same, That the Southerly Part of the said Town of Dedham be and hereby is set off and constituted a Separate Township by the Name of Walpole. The Bounds of said Township to be as follows viz: To begin at Dorchester Line where the Line of Wrentham intersects it and so to extend to Hawes's Brook, the said Brook to be Bounds till it comes to Bubling Brook, and on the same Course with Bubling Brook to Medfield Road, and so along the Road till it comes to Medfield Line and upon Medfield Line until it meets with Wrentham Line, and so upon Wrentham Line till it comes to the First Station, And that the Inhabitants of the said Lands as before described and bounded be and hereby are Vested with the Powers, Privileges and Immunities that the Inhabitants of any of the Towns of this Province by Law are or ought to be Vested with. Provided that the Inhabitants of the said Town of Walpole do within the space of Eighteen months from the Publication of this Act, Erect and Finish a suitable House for the Public Worship of God, and as soon as may be procure and settle a learned Orthodox Minister of good conversation, and make provision for his comfortable and honorable Support; And Likewise provide a School Master to Instruct their Youth in Writing and Reading, And that thereupon they be discharged from any further Payments for the Maintenance of the Ministry and School in the Town of Dedham. AND BE IT FURTHER ENACTED by the Authority aforefaid. That the Inhabitants of the said Town of Walpole, be and hereby are Impowered to Assess all the Lands of Non-Residents lying within the said Town One Penny per Acre towards the Charge of Building the Meeting House and Settling and Maintaining a Minister there. Anno Regni Regis Georgii Undesimo."

CHAPTER V

THE first entry in the Walpole town records is this:

"Att a meeting of the town of Walpole December ye 28, 1724 duly warned to Chuse Town officers, the Town Chose Ebenezer Fales to be moderator for the Meeting.

"It was Voted in the affirmative to Chuse Three Select Men and one Constable, at sd meeting the Town made Choice of Samuel Kingsbery to be Town Clerk and one of the selectmen, and Serj Joshua Clap & Serj Ezra Morse to be the other Two, and Chose John Hall Constable and att the same time the Town Clerk and Constable warre sworn before the Select men to the faithful Discharge of their ofices."

This appears to have been all the business transacted at our first town meeting. The doings of the second town meeting are recorded as follows:

"February ye 15, 1724-5 assembled the Select Men & they Nominated Daniel Morse to the Court of Excize as Sutable to Entertain Travelers."

This looks very much like some of our special town meetings of to-day. Of the third town meeting the record speaks thus:

"Att a Meeting of the Towne March ye 8, 1725 Duly warned for ye same Serg Ezra Morse was Chose moderator for the meeting. Samuel Kingsbery was Chose Town Clerk and one of the Selectmen. The others Were Serj. Joshua Clap, Serj. Ezra Morse, Ebenezer Falles, Joseph Hartshorn. Ebenezer Robins Chose Constable, upon refusal

Proceed and Chofe Thomas Clap, Conftable; Peter Fales, Senor, was Chofe Tithing man; John Boyden, Jedediah Morfe, Field Drivers; Peter Fales, Ezekiel Robins, Fence Viewers. Joshua Fisher, Thomas Hartshorn, Ezra Morfe were Chofe Serveirs for High ways. Eleazer Partridge, Samuel Shears, Hog Reaves.

"The faid officers were fumond by the Conftable to appear att the houfe of Jofhua Clap ye 12 of this Inftant, att five oClock at Night to be Sworn to the Faithful Difcharge of ther offices.

"on ye fd 12 of March asfembled the felect men att the Houfe of Joshua Clap and be sworn. Joshua Fisher, Thomas Hartshorn, Ezra Morfe, John Boyden, Jediah Morfe were fworn to the faithful Difcharge of ye offices they were Chofen to, and att fame Time Peter Fales Sen. Thomas Clap, Ezekiel Robins, Samuel Shears Refufed to be fworn to the faithful Discharge of their offices they were Chofe to."

Human nature then seems to have been pretty much as it is now. Some one failed to get the public notice he thought himself entitled to, which before the month was out led to the following meeting:

"Att a meeting of the Town March ye 30, 1725 Ebenezer Falles was Chofe Moderator for said Meeting, there being Difference Refpecting the meeting on the 8th of March Inftant. It was Propofed to the Town In written words viz if it be the Minds of the Town that thofe officers that were Chofen att meeting of the Town ye 8th of March Inftant, should Stand and Remain in their Ofices they were Chofe to then to Signifie it by Houlding up the hand, there not being a Major Vote upon it, the Moderator Proceeded to a New Choice — a Lift of the officers Chofen on faid Day. Samuel Kingsbery Chofen Town Clerk and one of the Select men. Peter Fales Sen. Ebenezer Fales, Thomas Clap, Joseph Hartshorn. Peter Fales Jun. Ezekiel Robins, Fence viewers. Said Peter Fales Chofe Town Treasurer; ebenezer Robins Chofe Conftable; John Hall Titheingman; Eleazer Partridge, John Guild, Hog Reaves; John Boyden, Jediah Morfe, Field Drivers; Joshua Fisher, Thomas Hartshorn, Ezra Morse Jun. Surveirs for High Ways.

"Att the above said meeting, this Town Granted fix Pound for the Defraying of Town Charges. And it was further Propofed to the Town to Raife money to build a meeting houfe upon the Place prefixd by the Generall Court which is near to Thomas Claps, and voted in the affirmitive.

"And att the fame meeting the Town Chofe a Commite to overfee and take care and manage the building ye sd meeting houfe, the Commite were Joshua Fisher, Ebenezer Fales, Thomas Clap, Joseph Hartshorn, Daniel Morfe. Att the fame meeting it was Propofed to Let the Swine go att Large, and Voted."

Six pounds for a town meeting's appropriation seems but the spectre of our constant experience. Even the early swine seem favored. The next town meeting appears to consider the question of our first Representative to the General Court of the Province. Dedham, the mother town, had always sent her best men.

"May ye 11, 1725, Asfembled ye Select men and apoynted a Town meeting to be upon the 18 of May Inftant to Chufe a Representative and to Confider further concerning Building the meeting houfe and to make it lefe if the Town sees Cause. Att a Meeting Dely warned for ye same Did upon Confideration agree. Att a meeting of the Town on the 18 of May 1725 Samuel Kingsbery was Chofe Moderator for sd meeting. The Town att ye sd meeting, agreed not to Chufe a Reprefentitive, and upon further Confideration did agree to build a Meeting Houfe Smaller than was Propofed and Voted att a meeting of the Town ye 30 of March in the year abovesaid, it was Voted in the affirmative to build a meeting houfe on the Place Perfixed by the General Court Near the Houfe of Thomas Claps 36 feet long & 30 foot wide & 18 foot ftud. The Town att the fame meeting Granted Fifty Pounds for the first Rate towards Building ye fame, and it was likwife Granted that the Inhabitants of the Town that Inclined fhould have Libberty to Labour in the Work of the fd Building onwards of their Part in the faid Fifty Pound, and fhall be allowed 3 fhillings and Six Pence a Day for a man and feven fhillings a Day for a man and Teame. And att the fame meeting the Town Chofe a Commite to Take Care and overfee with Refpect to the Building, and to agree with a workman as Refonably as they Can to affist in the Hewing and Framing and Finifhing fd Houfe, & the Commite are to take an Account of the Work of the Labourers and to give them Credit, Acording to their beft Judgment, the Commite Chofen the fame 18 of May Were Serg Joshua Clap, Ebenezer Fales, John Boreden, Joshua Fisher, Josep Hartshorn, Thomas Clap and Daniel Morfe."

Immediately following the above, this late item appears:

"Aprill ye 9, 1725 asfembled the felectmen and Chofe Ebenezer Fales and Thomas Clap to meet with Dorchester agents to Run the line and Renew the Bounds between Dorchester and Walpole."

As bearing on old localities the return of these men is most interesting, but to avoid repetition the one made a few years later and after this part of Dorchester had become Stoughton will suffice:

"A Journall of ye Marks in ye Line Between Walpole and Stoughton. On Aprill 29, 1734, Lt John Boyden and Jofeph Hartshorn being apointed Agents of ye Select men of the Town of Walpole to Run ye Line & Renew ye Bound marks of ye Line between Walpole and Stoughton Allfo John Hixfon and Charles Wentworth being apointed agents by the Town of Stoughton to Run ye faid Line. Perfuant to their orders, Repayrid to ye houfe of Capt. Morfe att ye Time apointed & Proceeded to the work of Preambulation, and be gan firft by Capt. Morfe at (3) Heeps of Stone — (ye (2) was a ftump Near ye Forge Pond, (ye 3) was a White Oak ftump (ye 4 was a white oak Neer ye River, (ye 5 a white oak Tree Near ye River, (ye 6 was a Stump with a heap of stones comonly called ye ftation Tree — ye 7 a Red oak Tree near a Swamp (ye 8 a Red Oak in ye Swamp (ye 9) a Hornbine in a Swamp ye 10 a Heep of ftones Near Carrels houfe — ye (11) a Maple tree in a Swale by ye Edg of ye Plain (ye 12 a Heap of ftones on a Ridg on high Plain (ye 13 a heep of ftones att a Root of a Pine fell down, ye 14 a heap of ftones Neer a flat Rock, ye (15 a Grey Oak in ye Edg of the Pine fwamp ye 18 a Heep of ftones by the Iron mine fwamp ye 19 a White Oak ye 20 a Great White Oak on a Ridg Neer ye Boxbufh (ye 21 a Heap of Stone on a Ridg Near a Road (ye 22 a White Oak in Bardens field (ye 23 a black Oak in a Ridg (ye 24 a black Oak (ye 25 a white Oak near a Great fwamp ye 26 a Heep of Stones (ye 27 a Great White Oak (ye 28 three Heeps of Stones ye 29 three Heeps of ftones more near ye Road (ye 30 a Heep of ftones on a Rock (ye 31 a Walnut ftub with a Heap of ftones (ye 32 a Heap of ftones on Raged Plain) ye 33 a Heap of ftones Neer ye high way (ye 34 a Heap of ftones on a Rock (ye 35 ye Great Rock ye Corner of Wallpole all ye aforefaid Trees markt with W. S."

The Captain Morse place was in the Morse neighborhood, Norwood; the Forge pond, the Frank Morse privilege; the River, the Neponset; the Carrol house, that of Joseph Carroll, part owner of Paige's farm; the High plain, the same as to-day, and the Pine Swamp the swamp north of Spring Brook; the Iron mine swamp, the swamp on the south side of Spring Brook; Boxbush, the swamp called now the peat meadow on the east side of Washington Street, a little to the south of the latter; the first Road, Common Street or the old Billings road; the Great swamp, Brush meadow; the next Road, the 1723 road by the old sawmill, now South Street; Raged Plain, the plain in extreme South Walpole; the great rock, the old bound known even to this day as Dedham Rock.

It must be remembered that Hawes Brook in Norwood, by Ellis pond and Morrill ink mill, was our northern boundary, and that the part of Dorchester east of our line had become a part of the new township of Stoughton.

In 1725 it became necessary to ascertain the taxable property in town:

"October ye 22, 1725 asſembled ye ſelectmen and apointed a Town meeting to be on the 29 of ſaid month to Chuſe ſome Town officers, and to agree with Reſpect to the hiring a miniſter, and for the Inhabitants to bring into the Selectmen a bill of their Eſtates. Att a Town meeting on the 29 of October 1725 Joshua Fisher was Choſe moderator and itt was voted in the affirmative to Chuſe one Selectman in the Room of Peter Fales Deceaſed. Att the same time Joshua Clap was Choſe to be one of the ſelectmen and att the ſame meeting the Town agreed to maintain Preaching among us for four months begining about the midle of November till the midle of March by free Contribution and Choſe a Comite to provide a miniſter, the Comite were Joshua Clap, Joshua Fisher, and William Robins."

At this early date something besides human beings sometimes got astray, we conclude from the following:

"January ye 17 1726 asſembled the ſelectmen and Choſe Ebenezer Fales to be Receiver of the Town money, and att the ſame time, the Select men agreed with Thomas Clap for a Convenient Piece of Land Near the Place for the meeting houſe to build a Pound on so long as the Pound shall be Capable of being Keep in Repair. Also agreed with Peter Fales to build a Pound about 40 feet long and 80 feet wide excepting ye Irons for 3 Pound five ſhilling and allso apoint a Town Meeting to be on the 7 of March to Chuſe Town officers and to conſider and do wt the Town may think fit with Reſpect to the Settling a miniſter and to agree to make the meeting houſe somethyng Larger than was Laſt Voted.

"At the meeting of the Town on the 7 of March 1726 Town officers were Choſen in the following order: Serg Ezra Morſe moderator; Samuel Kingsbury was Choſe Town Clerk & one of the Selectmen, the other Selectmen were Serj Joshua Clap, Serj Ezra Morſe, Joshua Fisher, John Boyden. Thomas Clap was Choſe Conſtable; Ebenezer Fales was Chofe Town Trefurer; Ezekiel Robins was Chofe Titheingman; John Guild, Moses Chamberlin, Field Drivers; Timothy Morfe, John Hall, Barnet Firrintun, Surveirs for High ways; William Jenks, James Borden, Fence Viewers; Robert Worfly, Samll Sheares, Hog Reaves.

"Att the fame meeting it was agreed to Chufe a Comite to Requeft the advice of fome of the Neighbouring Minifters with Refpect to the fettling and Choice of a minifter to fettle among us. Att a meeting of the Town on the 7 of March 1726, the Town Voted in the Affirmitive that the meeting houfe fhould be Built 2 foot Longer and 2 foot wider than what was Voted att a meeting of the Town on the 18 of May 1725.

"May ye 2, 1726 asfembled the felect Men and apointed a Town Meeting to be on the 19 of May Inftant to Confider and do what the Town shall think fit with Refpect to the Settling a minifter in this Town and to Grant money for the meeting Houfe and to Put it out by the Great or fome Part of it, and to grant money to Defray other Town Charges.

"Att a meeting of the Town of Wallpole on ye 19 of May 1726 the Town did then with the Advice of three of ye Neighbouring minifters elect and Chufe the Rev Mr. Joseph Belcher to Preach the Gospel & to Settle in the Work of the Miniftry among us. And att the fame meeting the Town Granted one Hundred Pound for Settlement of the faid Mr Joseph Belcher. Provided he be our ordained minifter. Fifty Pounds of it to be Paid the year he is ordained and fifty Pound of it the Next year after and for his falery the Town Granted for the Three frft years Fifty Pound a year, and after that Sixty Pound a year, and it was Voted in the afirmitive that the money on Written fhould be for Mr Belcher that comes in Contribution, and the Town Chofe Ebenezer Fales and Samll Kingsbery to Treat with the Reverend Mr Belcher."

The matter of the minister's salary was ever full of difficulty. But like the size of the meeting-house, there was at last an end.

"Att a meeting of the Town of Wallpole on ye 29 of June 1726 Duly Warned for the fame upon Further Confideration the Town Did alter

Somethings and Circomftances which Were Voted at a meeting of this Town on ye 19 of May 1726 viz. that fifty Pound of that which was then Granted at the abovefaid Meeting for ye Settlement of Mr Joseph Belcher fhall be Paid the fame year he gives his Anfwer. Provided it be given in the affirmative, and Fifty Pound of it the Next year after. And the Town Granted that the third year his falery fhould be Sixty Pound and the Forth year Seventy Pound and ye fifth year Eighty Pounds & when there Comes to be the Number of fifty-five Families Ninety Pounds a year, and the Town Granted to find him Fire Wood when he comes to Need it and the Town Granted that the Loofe money of the Neighbouring Inhabitants & Strangers money that may be Contributed fhall be for Mr. belcher over and above what is Ingaged as above faid, and Further it was Granted that he fhould have the ufe of the Lands that Lye in this Town that Belong to the Church in Dedham. Provided they can be obtained, and allfo that he fhall have what is Due from the Nonrefidents that have Dormant Lands in this Town by Virtue of the Court act, and it was Voted in the affermitive that Mr. Belcher should Continue with us to Preach the Gospel.

"And it was Voted to Petition the Town of Dedham for a Tract of Land Lying Between the Cedar Swamp and Wrentham Line for the Miniftry, and all so to Petition the Church in Dedham for their Lands Lyeing in this Town for the miniftry here, and the Town Chofe Ebenezer Fales, Joseph Hartshorn & Samuel Kingsbery to be a Commite to manage the Petitions. All so the Town att the fame meeting Chofe Ebenezer Fales to Tak Care of the Contribution.

"Att a meeting of the Town on the 19 of May 1726, the Town granted Fifty Pounds for the Building of meeting houfe, and all so the Town Voted in the affirmitive that in the Town Rates there be Ten Shilling set on the Poll in a fifty Pound Rate and fo Proportinally the Reft to be Levied on the Eftates.

"August 1726 Asfembled ye Select men & gave order to Ebenezer Fales Town Treasurer to Pay to John Richanfon Eleven Pound for what he did at ye meeting houfe, and att the fame Time gave order to the Trefurer to Pay to Samuel Kingfbery one Pound four fhilling for Books for ye Town."

The books referred to are those on which are now found our early records.

"September ye 27, 1726 asfembled the Select men and gave order to Ebenr Fales trefurer to Deliver Eight Pound for Nails for the meeting houfe.

December ye 9, 1725 affembled ye Selectmen and gave order to Ebenr Fales Trefurer to Pay to Peter Fales ye fum of Three Pounds five fhiling for Building ye Pound. December ye 14 1726, asfembled ye Select men and ordered Ebenr Fales, Trefurer to pay the Comite nineteen fhillings which they Paid to Mr. Richardfon for getting ye Timber for the Meeting houfe."

It seems that the Rev. Mr. Belcher had ministered to the spiritual wants of the town, though no record was made of his coming, as appears from the following action of the town:

"Att a meeting of ye Town on ye 19 of December 1726 the Town Voted in ye Afirmitive yt ye Select Men fhould Levy the fum of Eight Pounds thirteen fhilling and eight Pence for what was Due to Mr. Belcher fence the 29 of June laft, and allso granted fixteen Pounds for ye uphoulding the Preaching of the Gofpel among us and Chofe a Comite to Provid a minifter for ye Prefent, and to provid for his Entertainment. The Comite Chofen Were John Hall Ezekiel Robins and Daniel Morfe."

All meetings, whether religious or secular, were then held in private houses.

The first recorded assessment of the inhabitants of the town runs as follows:

"September ye 15, 1726. An asfesment made by us whofe Names are hereunto fubfcribed by Vertue of an Act of the General Court and warrent from this Province Treafurer. Wherein each Pertickler Perfons Proportion is Perfixt to their Names in Diftinct Colums:

	Polls		R. E.		P. E.	
Serg Joshua Clap	16	8	3	9	3	9
Serg Ezra Morſe	16	8	1	6	1	7
Ebenezer Falles	8	4	4	6	3	8
Joseph Hartshorn	16	8	2	3	ſ	3
John Boyden	12	6	2	3	ſ	3
Joshua Fisher	16	8	2	7	ſ	0
John Hall	16	8	2	3	ſ	2
William Robins	8	4	2	7	ſ	3
Thomas Clap	8	4	4	11	2	0
Timoth Morſe	8	4	3	0	0	8
John Guild	6	4	0	8	0	8
Barnerd Firuntun	8	4	ſ	1	0	9
Ebenezer Robins	8	4	2	7	1	3
Thomas Hartshorn	6	0	ſ	ſ	0	4
Ezra Morſe Jun	8	4	ſ	2	0	8
Samuel Pety	2	0	0	0	0	0
Daniel Sanders	6	0	0	0	0	0
William Fisher	8	4	0	5	0	5
John Marſh	4	0	0	0	0	0
Peter Fales	8	4	0	8	0	2
Roburt Allin	8	4	0	7	0	1
John Allin	8	4	0	7	0	0
William Jenks	8	4	5	7	0	6
Benjamin Elldridg	4	0	1	1	0	1
Stephen Clap	8	4	0	8	0	7
Samuel Shears	8	4	0	2	0	0
John Boyden	8	4	0	4	0	1
Eleazer Clap	8	4	0	0	0	0
Samuel Kingsbery	8	4	3	3	0	10
Ebenezer Turner	4	0	0	8	0	2
Eleazer Patridg	5	0	ſ	0	0	4
Ezekiel Robins	15	8	4	11	1	9
James Smith	8	4	ſ	10	0	0
Daniel Morſe	8	4	ſ	7	0	7
Jedidiah Morſe	8	4	0	9	0	0
James Bardens	4	0	0	2	0	4
Josiah Morſe	8	4	0	0	0	1
Moſes Chamberlain	6	4	0	2	0	3

	Polls		R. E.		P. E.	
William Patridge	8	4	0	5	0	0
William Foster	8	4	0	0	0	0
Joseph Parker	8	4	0	0	0	0
Nehemiah Ward	8	4	0	0	0	1
Beriah Ware	8	4	0	0	0	0
Wido Abigail Fales	0	0	2	3	0	10
John Allin Med	0	0	0	9	0	0
John Turner	0	0	0	11	0	0
Edward Turner	0	0	0	7	0	0
Henery Adams	0	0	0	2	0	0
Johnathan Boyden	0	0	0	4	0	0
James Fales	0	0	1	6	0	0
Dr. James Jero	0	0	0	9	0	0
John Buckmaster	0	0	0	9	0	0
Benjamin Allin	0	0	0	5	0	0
John Bullerd	0	0	0	5	0	0
Joseph Boyden	0	0	0	7	0	0
Benjamin Morfe	0	0	0	9	0	0
Samuel Clark	0	0	1	4	0	0
Henery Smith	0	0	0	7	0	0
Nathanill Guild	0	0	0	2	0	0
Wido Mary Chenery	0	0	0	9	0	0
Ifaac Chenery	0	0	0	7	0	0
Cap. Johnathan Boyden	0	0	0	9	0	0
Robart Worfly	2	0	0	0	0	0
John Morfe	8	4	0	0	0	0

Samuel Kingsbery
John Boyden } *Selectmen.*
Joshua Fisher

It will be noticed that the above list includes many non-residents and also leaves out many who lived in present Walpole territory — such as John Bullard, Isaac Lewis, Jeremiah Gould, Nathaniel Coney, and others.

In 1726 the first action is taken for support of the poor, as follows:

"and att the fame time gave sd Clap a warrant forthwith to pay into ye said Treafurer twenty shillings for the Ufe of ye Poor of said Town for his Giving in a falfe Bill for his Eftate to ye Select men."

In 1727 Ebenezer Fales and Thomas Clap were chosen at the March meeting to find a convenient place for the "Settlement for a Minifter." Joshua Fisher was also a member of the committee, but his name does not appear on either of the deeds made necessary in the purchase of the old Peter Fales place, the place thus purchased for a parsonage.

The following contributed either labor or money in the erection of the first meeting-house, as appears from the following:

"January ye 20, 1727 Asfembled ye Select Men and gave order to the Town Trefurer to Pay to feverall Perfons for work and other necefaries they did for the Meeting houfe

	£	s.	d.		£	s.	d.
To Samuel Kingsbery	0	12	11	To Robart Allin	1	2	5
To John Boyden	2	7	6	To Abbigaill Fales	1	18	1
To Jediah Morfe	0	8	7	To Ebenezer Fales	8	15	11
To Ezekiel Robins	2	2	2	To Nehemiah Ward	0	4	6
To Joshua Fisher	2	7	9	To George Allin	0	3	6
To Eleazer Patridge	0	11	4	To John Allin	0	8	0
To Ebenezer Turner	1	0	3	To Barnert Firintun	0	4	2
To Moses Chambelin	0	12	3	To Daniel Morfe	1	12	10
To Joseph Hartshorn	0	9	1	To Mr. Richardfon	14	5	0
To Thomas Hartshorn	0	10	0	To Timothy Morfe	2	0	0
To Joshua Clap	3	13	6				

The next entry in the early town records of interest is the following:

"Att a meeting of ye Town of Walpole on ye 7th of March 1727 it was Voted in the affirmitive to Choofe a Commite to Gather fome

Certain ſums of Money that have been ſubſcribed by ſome of ye Inhabitants of this Town as may apear by a ſubſcription towards ye Building of the meeting houſe and ſettling a miniſter, and they are to ſubduct out of ye ſame ſuch ſums as they ye Subſcribers, or others have Paid Towards ye Getting The Town ſet off by the Court. The Comitte Choſen Were Thomas Clap Samuel Kingsbery — And ye Comitte are to Pay the above ſaid money into the Town Treſurer."

The meeting-house all this time was slowly building, but another appropriation was, it seems, needed:

"Att a Meeting of ye Town on ye Seventh of March 1727, ye Town Granted Fifty Pound towards Finiſhing the Meeting houſe. On March ye 31 asſembled ye Select men and Gave order to ye Town Treſurer to Pay to Ebenezer Robins For Geting ſhingicles and Clabords for ye Meeting houſe ye ſum of 6 15 0. To Thomas Clap for Work and other Neceſaries ye sum of 2 9 9. To Joseph Carrel for Work 0 17 0. To Peter Fales for Work 0 4 6. To Samll Shears for Work 0 3 6. To William Jenks 2 9 10."

This is followed by an almost positive intimation that the people had at last got ready to permanently settle a minister and were dissatisfied with temporary makeshifts.

"Att a Meeting of ye Town of Walpole on ye Tenth of Aprill 1727 ye Town Granted Sixty Pound for the Uphoulding of ye Preaching of ye Gospel among us, and whereas Timothy Morſe Declined ſerving as a ſelectman, Joseph hartſhorn was choſen in his Room and ſtead att ye above ſaid meeting, and att ye ſame meeting, Thomas Clap, Ebenezer Robins & Ezekiel Robins Were Choſen for a Comite to provide a miniſter for ye Preſent. Sept. ye 29 1727 asſembled ye Select Men and apointed a town meeting to be on the fourth of October next to Grant money & to Grleaze the meeting houſe, and to Grant money to Defray Town Charges."

"And allfo att the fame time Gave order to Ebenezer Fales Trefurer to Pay to Mr. Joseph Belcher ye fum of 8 13 6. And allfo to Pay to ye Commite Viz John Hall, Daniel Morfe, Ezekiel Robins for Procuring Preaching in the Winter feafon In the year 1726 ye fum of £16."

It seems from this that most of the going to meeting then was done in the winter when the farmer could do but little else. It, however, had an advantage over the present custom of not going at all.

There next follows another list of townsmen who additionally helped to build our first meeting-house, and it must be remembered that the house was to be not merely a church but a place of general gathering:

"September ye 29, 1727 asfembled ye felect Men and Gave order to the Town Treafurer to Pay to the feverall Perfons under Writen for Work and Matterals For the Meeting houfe the feverall fums That are Perfixt to Their Names as Followeth:

	£	s.	d.
Joshua Clap	11	8	6
William Jenks	3	10	2
John Richardfon	1	14	6
Samuel Kingsbery	0	12	3
John Boyden	2	0	3
James Blake	6	14	6
Thomas Clap	2	12	0
Ephraim Clark	0	2	6
Jedidiah Morfe	1	4	0
Daniel Morfe	0	2	9
Thomas Lawrence	5	9	0
Eleazer Patridge	0	14	0
John Hall	1	0	0
William Robins	0	4	0
Barnert Firintun	0	10	0
Samuel Pety	0	12	8
John Boyden, Jr	4	1	6
Mofes Chamberlin	0	9	6
Joseph Hartshorn	0	7	0
John Guild	0	7	0
Ebenezer Fales	24	14	5
Samuel Toplif	12	10	0
Heirs of Edward Wiatt	6	5	0
Peter Lyon	0	17	6
Thomas Hartfhorn	0	7	0
James Smith	0	1	10
Timothy Morfe	0	9	6

"January ye 16, 1728. Asfembled ye Select Men and Gave order to ye Town Treafurer to Pay to ye Comitee Viz Tomas Clap, Ebenezer

Robbins, Ezekiel Robins ye fum of Twenty-nine Pound for their Procuring Preaching Twenty faboths."

Besides the condition that the town should establish preaching, there was also, in the act of incorporation, one that it should support a school. Year after year went by while it was struggling with the ministerial question, until something turned their attention to their continued neglect of this important matter, as thus appears:

"February ye 16 1728 asfembled ye Select men and Gave order for a Town Meeting to be on the fifth of March to Chufe Town officers and to Grant money to Defray the Town Charges, and allso to Grant money for a fchool, and for the Town to manifest their Minds with Refpect to the fettling Mr belcher."

At the March meeting in 1728 the town voted to reduce the number of selectmen to three,— Ezra Morse, Joshua Fisher, and Samuel Kingsbury; the latter also being continued as Town Clerk, as Ebenezer Fales was continued Treasurer. At this meeting a new town official was chosen called "furveier of fhingle and Clabord," the high honor going to Joseph Hartshorn.

"It was also voted that the town brand in the future should be WA, and that the meeting should be adjourned until the 16th of April to renew the call to Mr Belcher and to choose Ebenezer Fales and Samuel Kingsbery to secure the services of Mr Belcher untill then."

On April 16, 1728, the town voted to accept their proportion of the sixty thousand pounds of the General Court of the Province, and appointed Ezra Morse, Sr. Ezra Morse, Jr., and Joseph Morse the trustees, who engaged to pay into the treasury of the Province both principal and interest as the law directed, and also to pay interest to the treasurer of the town for the use of the town after the rate of one pound per cent annually, for which they gave sufficient bond. But with all their need of expedition with their meeting-house, when a motion was made for the old committee to continue building the result was an emphatic "non-concurrence," followed by the only hopeful occurrence, in the following August, of paying the account of Joshua Clap, fifteen shillings for boarding the minister.

On April 16, 1728, the town voted to settle the Rev. Joseph Belcher and received this acceptance:

"Walpole, May 17, 1728 — To the Inhabitants of Walpole — Sirs: I Defire to be duely fencible of the Importance of The Work and fervice unto Which you have fo kindly Invited me among you, and I am fencible That it is an afair Which Requireth great Deliberation and ferious Thought, and who Indeed is fuffishent for Thefe Things, I Hope I have Taken the Call which I Receaved from you to fettle In the Work of the Miniftry among you into ferious Confideration, and I Hope I have endeavoured to Delibrate Thereupon with folemity, ferioufnefs and affection, and I hope and Truft I have had the Divine Derection in the Methods of Piety Together with the Councell and Advice of Able and Wife Judges with Refpect to my Proceeding in the Weighty affairs before me, I would Endeavour to Confider and Take Notice of the Providence of God in your Electing and Calling me to settle in the Work of the Miniftry among you, and in your Renewing the call of Late, and I am Perfuaded Thatt divine Providence Calls and Oblidges me to an acceptance. Wherefore Thankfully accepting your call to Settle ie the Work of Ministry among you my anfwer Thereto is in the Affirmitive in Which I Defire Willingly and Sincerely to give up myself to the Service of Chrift in the gospel among you. Depending upon Divine help and affiftance. Hoping you Will nott be wanting Hereafter in your kindnefs and Encoragements Towerds me, and fo be fpeaking To Joyn with me in Sincere and fervant Prayers to god, for his Gracious affiftance, Bleffing and Direction in the Important Afair before us I fubferib my felf your Servant in Offices of Duty and Love.

"JOSEPH BELCHER."

It was intimated in general language of Mr. Belcher's call, that the town would purchase or in some way obtain the Dedham Church lands for the use and benefit of the ministry, but in acceptance of the call, on another occasion, Mr. Belcher kindly released the town therefrom.

CHAPTER VI

THE same year the town ran all its lines, and both the old names of Bubbling Brook and Hawes Brook, with the additional interesting local history, appear:

"June 1728 afsembled ye Select Men and apointed thatt the ferveirs fhould mend the high waye, as followeth: That William Fifher fhould Take care of them from ye fence Parting Thomas hartfhorns Land from Halls to Dedham Line, and that Eze. Robins fhould Take Care of them from fd fence to Mofes Chambelins, and the faid Chambelin fhall take care of them from Thence to ftop River."

The first mention of payment of town officers appears in the following:

"Feb. ye 21, 1729 afsembled ye Select men & gave order to ye Town Tressurer to Pay to Samll Kingsbury fifteen fhilling for Wrighteen for ye Town."

Up to this date the penmanship of the early records, pretty much all done by this man, is deserving of all praise, neat and legible, which cannot be said of that of his successor in the town clerkship, Ezra Morse, Jr. That closely approaches the well-scratched ground of a busy hen yard. The next vote was to allow the swine to run at large. May 5, there was, also, the matter of accepting the resignation of the Rev. Joseph Belcher, the fencing the burial yard, and running the road below the forge over the forge dam. Seventeen pounds and fourteen shillings were ordered paid to Jonathan Billings for "glafing the meeting houfe."

At the following May meeting it was proposed to lay out a road from Sawmill road by the house of Ezra Morse to the Stoughton line. This was Mylod Street, which for years after was called the Lieut. Ezra Morse road.

The town voted that they would dismiss Mr. Belcher from being their minister and to pay him one hundred pounds by the seventeenth of that month. Again the town refused to choose a Representative.

On the following fifteenth the town appropriated £80 to have preaching again, and John Hail, Ezekiel Robins, and Thomas Hartshorn were chosen to secure a minister in place of Mr. Belcher, but refused to grant any money to finish the meeting-house. This year the names of Isaac Lewis, John Bullard, and Joseph Willet first appear on the Walpole tax list.

On Sept. 22, 1729, the town voted to settle another minister at once. Several, including Phillips Payson of Dorchester, a graduate of Harvard College in the class of 1724, had appeared as candidates. The fourth motion at this meeting runs thus:

"it was propofed to the town warther Mr payfon fhould be the firft in nomination and it was voted in the afermitive, it was propofed to the Town warther Mr Joseph baxtar Junr. fhuld be the fecond in nominaton and voted in the afarmitive. 6ly it was propofed to the Town warther Mr Bowles should be the third in nomination and voted in the afarmitive. And it was propofed to the town warther they woud have Mr Messenger, Mr Dexter or Mr Buckman and Mr Dunbar tree of tham to carre on the fast."

This is followed by another and conclusive entry:

"Att a Meting of the Town Octtober the 20, 1729 the Town made choice of Mr phillips payson to be thare minifter by 30 votes and Mr Joseph baxter Junor by 7 votes. It was propofed to the town wather thay would give Mr payfon the fome of one hundred pounds fertlement provided he be our ordained minifter and voted in the afermitive. itt was propofed to the town wather thay would give Mr payfon the fome of one hundred pounds salary a year fo long as he fhall be our minifter voted in the afermitive. Ebenezer falef, John bordens famuale kingf-bury committemen to prefent thar cafe to Mr payfon."

In the following February, the weather forced them to also grant their minister the firewood he had months before requested in his letter of acceptance. This chapter of the records ends with the following:

"Febr. ye 27, 1728 the Selectmen ordered the Town Treafurer to pay to Ebenezer Turner ye fum of Twenty fhilling and to William Holden the like fum of Twenty fhilling for killing Two Grown Wild Cats."

This was the first chance for any but the officials to get anything out of the town treasury.

At the March meeting of 1730 the town appropriated thirty pounds to finish the meeting-house, which had been going to be finished for the last five years, but still had failed to get there.

Following this entry is another reference to early localities:

THE FIRST MEETING-HOUSE OF WALPOLE, THE CHURCH OF THE REV PHILLIPS PAYSON, SR.

Situated on the west central part of the old Meeting-House Common, Walpole Centre. The hill was afterwards removed for a site for the second meeting-house

"On ye 30 of March 1730 Asſembled ye Selectmen and appointed Joseph Hartshorn surveir to Take care of and mend the high ways in Walpole from Dedham Line as far as to ye South east of Ebenr Fales and Benjan Carrels and the Hands within the ſaid Bounds. And allſo appointed Joſhua Clap ſurveir to Take care of and Mend the Ways In Walpole from Ebenr Fales and Ben Carrols as far as a Hill in ſaid Town called and known by the Name of the Diged Hill and to have the hands within the ſaid Bounds. And Allſo apointed Ephraim Clark to Take of and Mend the high ways in Walpole from the Diged Hill to the Wrentham Lyne with the hands within the ſaid Bounds."

On June 19, 1730, a day of fasting and prayer, on a "Thursday in July," was appointed, at which three of the neighboring ministers were to assist. It was further voted to have the new minister, Phillips Payson, ordained Wednesday, September 9 following, and that on August 19 they should hold a meeting at their meeting-house to arrange for the ordination; and it was voted, also, that

"Ye entertainment ſhould be made att ye houſe of Ebenezer Fales, he conſenting to Take it att 5 shilling a man, Samuel Austing Jeremiah Day, John Guild and Jacob Ellis were chosen to Preſerve ſeverall ſeats which were mentioned for the Elders and Meſſingers and Church."

The ordination was deferred, however, at the request of Mr. Payson, until September 16.

This is followed by:

"On ye 16 of September, the Rev. Mr. Philips Payson was ordained Pastor to the Church of Walpole."

This year weights and measures were procured for the town—brass weights from one ounce to four pounds, scales, beer quart, wine pint, wine half pint, gill pot, half bushel, peck and half peck, a brand and stamp, and a yard.

March, 1731, fifty pounds more were appropriated for the long finishing meeting-house. In 1732 one pound was paid Samuel Petty for right of highway through his land. On March 17, 1732, the town granted

"30 Pound for ye upholding of schools, in ye Town 15 Pound of it to be Improved for ye Inftructing ye Litle Children in ye fumer Time to be for a woman School and to be Improved in Maner following Namely att Eafy Plain and Near ye Meeting houfe, and about a mile or a mile and half Northeaft ard of ye fame where the Select men fhall appoint. The other 15 Pound to be Improved for Writing School In the Wintr feafon to be for a moveing School to be kept att ye a bove mentioned Places as Each Part to have their Equall Proportion of Time.

"Att ye Same Meeting it was Voted in ye afermitive to bring In the Minifter's Salary in Way of Contribution, and that Thofe Perfons that fhall bring in their money In this Method Writing on their Money and Putting it in to ye Contribution Box fhall have it of fett in the Minifter Rate. Ebenezer Fales was Chofe to Take care of ye Box.

"Att ye same Meeting the Town axcepted of a Highway Laid out by John Boyden and Samuel Kingsbury by order of ye felectmen Laid out Two Rods wide and Mark on ye North fide of ye fame on severall small Treefs and a ftake from the High way Near a Bridg Called Rams Bridg to ye Bridg by Morfes Mill att Stop River."

On April 10, 1732, the town voted to join the neighboring towns in forming a new county, and Lieut. Ezra Morse was chosen to represent them in the matter.

"Sept 22 asfembled ye Select men & Deputed Capt Esra Morfe, Lt John Boyden and Mr Joseph Hartshorn to Vew and Lay out, If they fee Caufe, a High way from ye Rhoad in Walpole By ye Buring Place to ye Houfe of Joseph Carrel Where it may be Moft Benefeciall to ye

Publict and Leaft Damage to Propriety and they are to make Return to ye Town ye Next Annual Meeting."

In March, 1733, the first school-teachers received their pay,— James Kingsbury and Mary Hall for teaching at Easy or Walpole Plain.

March 6, 1733, appears the following:

"It was allfo Voted In ye affamitive to Choufe a Commite to Vew and allter ye Road Near Brufh Meadow upon William Partridges Land if they think fit Provided ye faid Partridge fhall Mak ye Road good and Paffible att his own Charge to ye Acceptation of ye Committee. Ye Committee chofen were Thomas Clap, Daniel Morfe Enf Clap.

"Ye Town Granted to Ezekiel Robbins for Looking after ye Meeting houfe and Sweeping it 3 year and a half 3 10 0 and to Samuel Kingsbury for Writing for ye Town ye year 1732, Twenty shiling."

Then appears the following reference to the portion of East and Kendall streets referred to above:

"March ye 1, 1733 asfembled ye Select men & laid out a High Way from fhinkins [Simpkins] Land by Joseph Carrols Houfe to ye Rhoad by the Burying Place Two Rod wide & markt as followeth; being Within one Rod on ye fouth fide of William Fosters Houfe from thence to a ftub Markt (2) a walnut Tree ye (3) a Gray oak and Turning foutherly to black Burch and fo to Daniel Fishers Land as ye Trees are Markt. Then Turning Westerly upon ye Line Between Dec. Fales and Daniel Fisher's Land Dec. Fales has given one Rod Till itt comes to the Northweft corner of Daniel Fifhers fence & then 3 Gray Oaks being Markt on ye North fide of ye Rhoad, and through Mr Halls Land as it is Markt ye faid Hall giving ye Land, And from thence over ye brook to Churches Land as ye Road is now drawn. Dec. Fales giving the Land, and when it comes to ye Land called Churches to Continue wher it is now Drawn Till itt Comes to the Road by the Burying Place fo to Continue Till fuch Time as Decon Fales and William Robbins do agree upon and ſtate a Line between them in that Place & when they agree upon that Matter they Have Promiſed each of them to give a Rod wide on their Line Till it comes to the Road aforeſaid which ye ſaid Fales and Robbins have Promiſed before ye Select men."

It is interesting to note more particularly the expenditures in finishing the meeting-house. Obadiah Morse received 2 pounds for "irons"; John Snow, Sr., 26 pounds 7 shillings for labor; Joseph Hartshorn, 2 pounds 10 shillings; James Blake, for 735 feet of boards and carting, 3 pounds 7 shillings; James Smith, for nails; Samuel Morse for "springs"; Peter Lyon, for sawing, 2 pounds 4 shillings; Jonathan Wight, for carting a load of boards from Wrentham to the meeting-house, 2 shillings; Joshua Fairbank, for a thousand feet of boards for the meeting-house, 5 pounds; Ezekiel Robbins, for part payment of workmen's board, 3 pounds.

May 30, 1733, twenty pounds were appropriated for finishing the still unfinished meeting-house.

In 1734 the town authorized Capt. Morse and Lieut. Boyden to purchase a stock of powder and bullets. Jacob Ellis was chosen surveyor of the new road from bubling brook to Wrentham road. Joseph Willet of the ways on the north east side of Spice and Mill Brooks; Henry Smith of the way from the sandy hill by Ezekiel Robbins to Stop River with the hands at Easy Plain, he allowing John and Jonathan Boyden to do their proportion of work in the new road across their land; Stephen Clap for the rest of the ways southeast of Spice and Mill brooks. The town also arranged with William Fisher to furnish fifteen pounds' worth of firewood at eight shillings a cord

THE ISAAC LEWIS, SR.—JOHN LEWIS—CHARLES EVERETT PLACE

Owned for a few years by both William Foster and Joseph Coney. The birthplace of Rev. John Lewis, husband of the Rev. Harlan Page's only daughter; also the birthplace of Fanny S. Lewis, eighteen years missionary to India as wife of the Rev. H. M. Scudder of Brooklyn, N. Y. The Rev. John Lewis was also one of our early school-teachers

for their pastor. Deacon Fales still had charge of the contribution box.

The above mentioned new road in the north part of the town is thus described:

"A Rhoad Laid out by Capt. Morse, Joseph Hartshorn and Thomas Clap Feb. 25, 1733. Laid out 2 Rods wide from Bubling brook between the land of Eleazer bulerd and James Jero so far as their Land goes, from thence to the House of Moses Elice as strait as may be & from sd Jacobs House to Nathaniel Gays Frame as it is markt out and from Gays Frame to the house of Jeremiah Day as straight as may be & from said Days to Wrentham Rhoad as strait as may be between John Halls and Thomas Hartshorns. The above said Rhoad was Proposed and Excepted by the Town at their Aniversary meeting In March 1734."

This was North Street and was followed by the two mentioned below:

"A Rhoad Laid out by the Select men Nov 5, 1733, Cross a part of Sawmill Devident Begining att the North side of Jonathan Boydens Land as itt is Drawn till it Comes by his house to a White Oak Tree Marked, then running on John Boydens Land on a Ridg hill til it comes to a small Pine, from thence to a Red Oak from thence to the corner of his fence and so to his Frame as straight as may be & so to Stoughton Line. And allso from the White Oak above mentioned between Jonathan and Johns Land till itt comes to Huppers and so between them, each allowing a Rod and till itt comes to Gays Land and upon itt as itt is now Drawn till itt Comes to a Walnut Tree markt, so to a black oak, and so by the Maks till itt comes to Stoughton Line. Proposed and accepted by the Town March 5 1734."

The first mention of any payment for teaching in the north part of the town occurs as follows:

"On March 4, 1735 ye Select men ordered Ebenezer Partridg Const to Deliver and Pay to Joseph Hartshorn 7 12 0 five Pound thereof to Pay for ye School which has been keept att Petties & 2 12 of it to Pay for School Keept in ye midle of ye Town."

This year Jedediah Morse was paid for sawing lumber and plank for two bridges, and Lieut. John Boyden for laying out a way to Scratch Hollow.

An attempt was made, the same year, to allow the public to construct pews in the meeting-house at their own expense and regard them their own property, but it did not succeed. It was, however,

"Agreed yt there ſhould be a Board Put Round ye houſe ſutable for ye Time. Plaiſtering to come too below and yt ye ſeats in ye Gallery be made, and the walls ſeald with board att ye back of ye ſeats in ye Gallery as high as may be ſutable, and ye Reſt of ye Walls and allſo on ye beams Plaiſterd with Lime."

The everlasting finishing the meeting-house, however, seems to have been puzzling them still. At this meeting occurs the first mention of jurors when

"the town voted that Joshua Fishers Name ſhould be Left out of ye Box of Petty Jurors Provided he Pay forty ſhilling towards finiſhing ye meeting Houſe, the doing of which ſhall free him from ye ſervice by Reaſon of his bodily weakness. The ſd forty ſhilling has been Paid."

This year the name of Jeremiah Dexter, probably connected with the Dedham Dexters, first appears. The Medfield road was also improved and straightened.

Even in 1736, twelve years after the incorporation of the town, the meeting-house finishing was still quietly going on, as appears from the following entry:

"Choſe John Hall, John Guild, Ebenezer and Ezekiel Robins and

Joshua Clap a Committee to Manage the finifhing the Meeting Houfe, and it was a Greed on yt Thofe Perfons That fhall Putt money Into the Contribution Box on Saboth Days and Write on their money fhall have it offfet in their Rates att years Ende."

In 1736 appear the names of Eben Baker, George Cleaveland, and Samuel Copp. In 1737 Thomas Clap was paid for "Looking after ye meeting houfe," and Ebenezer Robins for "Providing timber & Sawing & Drawing yt along," indicating that since settlement there had been three sawmills in town Samuel Kingsbury, who was Town Treasurer, also at the same time acted as a teacher in the public schools, which continued to be kept on the Plain, in the Centre and at the east part of the town.

There is so much interesting early history in the first assignments to road surveyors, the following is added:

"The felect Men asfembled March 24, 1737 and agreed & ordered that Daniel Smith Surveir fhould Take Care & mend the Roads Leading from Stop River to Spice brook & to have ye Hands att Eafye Plain Sam Shears, Peter Fales Eze Robins Thomas Clap Aquilla Robins Jofiah Morfe and thofe Dwelling with them. And yt Roburt Allin fhould Have ye care of ye Reft of ye Ways on ye fame fide of faid brook & have ye Reft of ye hands on faid fid of ye brook. And that William Fifher fhould take Care of ye Road Leading from ye Road Neear Huppers to bubbling brook and to have Petitioners for faid Way to Mend ye fame. And that Jofeph Morfe with ye Reft of ye Hands on ye Northerly fide of ye faid brook take care of and Mend the Reft of ye Roads on ye faid fide of ye brook. And att ye fame time gave ye Conftable Warrant to order a perfon Refident att Aldritches to Depart out of ye Town, his Name is attwood."

This year Henry Smith and Ensign Clap were chosen a committee to provide "School Dames."

That the meeting-house was not yet "quite" finished appears from the town's action on June 21, 1738, when it voted to "Defer ye Plaiftering on the Beams in the Meeting houfe till further order." It also voted that there should be "two Pews Made att ye Towns Charge to be for the Towns ufe on the Northeafterly end of the Pulpit," and that "the Remainder of the room Defigned for Pews fhould be Granted to thofe Perfons thatt fhall appear and make them on their own Charge for their ufe and feats in ym making this Provife that in cafe any Perfons fhould fe caufe to fell their Pews that the Town fhould have the offer of them and alfo voted that they fhould have their choice fucceffively acording to their Bills of Eftates, and Left the Ordering of the Matter to the Selectmen."

At the meeting, July 13, 1738, it was voted that there should be eight pews made in the room designed for pews in spite of the following:

"On the 30 June 1738. Asfembled ye Selectmen and thought fitt and agreed that the room in ye meeting houfe Defigned for Pews that was Granted to Perfons that would build them att their own Charge fhould be made into twelve Pews, viz: Six on the Southeaftly fide of the houfe and three att the fouthweft end and three att the Northeaft End of the Houfe.

"The moft of the Perfons being Prefent that were to make their Choice Proceeded to choofe as followeth Thomas Clap chofe on ye Right hand Next ye Great doars, Next Joyninge to that William Robins chofe, on the Left hand Next the Great doars, Dec. Ebenezer Fales chofe, Next Joyning to that Jofeph Hartfhorn chofe, Next Joyning to that Jacob Elice Chofe, on the Left hand going in att the Southwest Doar enfign Jofhua Clap Chofe, the Next Joyning to that Ebenezer Robbins Chofe, the Next joyning to that Ezekiel Robins Chofe."

It has always been held at the Secretary of State's office, where there is a copy of the earliest map of the Town, that of 1794, that the meeting-house there represented is that of the second edifice, and that the first faced to the northwestward, and that the surveyor in his diagram indicated the change from that direction towards the northeast. The roof is most peculiar.

The house is there placed on the northeasterly corner of the junction of the old Wrentham Road and a street running southeasterly through the middle of what is now the Common.

This conforms with tradition coming down to the author, and the southwest door mentioned above seems to corroborate it. This was the southwestwardly side door on the old Wrentham road.

This year Nathaniel Guild, John Hooper, and Jedediah Morse of Stoughton asked to join their lands to the town of Walpole, and "Barnard Faringtun was supported by the town through a long sickness." Also Ezra Morse and his sons petitioned the General Court to be set off to Dedham.

Also the owners of pew rights relinquished them on condition that the town would, at its own expense, build eight pews. Only Ebenezer Fales and Thomas Clap had prepared for the construction of their pews. Their boards and labor were compensated for by the town.

John Guild and Jonathan Lawrence were the school-teachers this year and the people were, by a committee, seated in the meeting-house.

On May 21, 1739, the town voted to give Mr. Payson twelve pounds in money, in lieu of firewood. The pastor was then living in the place purchased in 1727, by the committee, Ebenezer Fales and Thomas Clap above referred to, from the heirs of Peter Fales, Sr., for the settlement of the minister, to whom it had been conveyed in 1732, just before his marriage to Anne Swift, daughter of Rev. Mr. Swift of Framingham. This house was standing till destroyed by fire a few years ago. For many years it was owned in equal shares by Jason Ellis, our old undertaker, and James G. Hartshorn, and was the house next north of the estate of Deacon Bradford Lewis.

As late as 1739 the usual annual appropriations, with the exception of the minister's and teachers' salaries, were some ten pounds.

Aug. 24, 1739, for a variety, Benjamin Perkins was warned out of town, and schoolhouses engaged some much needed attention.

"November ye 6, 1739 voted in the afirmitive that the Town would build three ſchool houſes and that each Part of the Town ſhould build their own houſe at their own Charge. One Neare William Fiſhers houſe, ſecond school houſe on Leu. Clap Land on Northeast ſid of the Road Leading to billings Neare the road going to the fourge — the third on ye Land of Deacon Kingsbery on that ſid of his Lot next Dextors on the left hand of the road and the Town granted Ten pounds for a school for the winter ſeaſon to be in the middle of the Town."

In 1738 Thomas Clap had endeavored to get the town to secure a title to the meeting-house site, concerning which the following bond had been previously given:

"April ye 4 1737 Asſembled the ſelectmen upon the Desire of Thomas Clap and agreed with him as follows —

"Know all men by theſe preſents that I Thomas Clap of Walpole in ye County of Suffolk, and province of Masfachusetts bay in New England, yoman, am Holden and ftand Bound and obliged unto John Boyden Jofeph Hartfhorn Jofhua Fifher Jofhua Clap and Daniel Smith all of ye Town and County aforefaid and felect Men of ye faid Town of Walpole in ye full and Just fum of five Hundred pounds lawfull money of New England to be paid unto ye faid Select Men or their fuccefers in faid Truft for the uses and Benefit of faid Town To the which payment well and Truly to be made I bind myfelf my Heirs, Executors, adminiftrators and Every of them firmly by thofe prefents. fealed with my feal Dated ye Forth Day of April AD. 1739 and in ye Twelvth year of his Majefties Reign Gorg ye fecond King &c.

"The Condition of ye Above obligation is fuch that whereas ye meeting houfe in faid Walpole now ftands on ye land of the above bounden Thomas Clap and he having agreed to give ye Town of Walpole aforefaid ye use benifit and Improvement of all ye land without his fence on each fide of fd meeting houfe fo long as fd Town fhall fee Cafe to Improve the fame as it is now Improved and to build and Rebuild meeting houfes on ye fd land and no other building in Confideration that ye Town of Walpole Do at a Town meeting of fd Town Duly warned before ye firft day of June Next voat and grant unto ye fd Thomas Clap ye Next pue to ye foutherly Door of ye Meeting houfe on ye Right hand of faid Door for him and his familys ufe or Choufe a comitie at faid meeting that fhall pay or caus to be paid or Duly tendered unto ye faid Thomas Clap ye fum of Ten pounds in your Bills of Credit of ye old Tenier within six months from faid meeting.

"Now Therfore if ye fd Town Do grant faid pue as aforsfaid or fd Comitee fo Chofen or any other purfon Do pay or Tender faid fums of Ten pounds to ye fd Clap and ye faid Clap Thereupon giving to fd Town a good and ample writing to be provided by fd felect Men or Comitee according to ye Tru Intent and meaning of ye above Recited agreement that may be fufficient to Convay and make fure ye fame as aforefaid then ye above Writen obligation to be vid and of none affect other wife to ftand and remain in full force.

"Thomas Clap

"figned fealed and Delivered In Presents of us

"Peter Lyon William Wright"

CHAPTER VII

AT the opening of cold December, 1739, in spite of weather or feeling, the town records:

"Walpole December ye 3, 1739 — by order of a Warrant from the felectmen Jofeph petty and mary petty his wife were warned out of this town as the Law Directs."

As a just punishment one Hannah Pettee afterwards obliged the town to support her for life.

Among the citizens of this year appears what may be taken for our first acquisition from Bonnie Scotland or the Emerald Isle, "Nail Macknail." He may have been Scotch. Whether Scotch or Irish, he, like all the other inhabitants, contributed his share towards the minister's salary.

In 1740 an attempt was made to lay out what is now Fisher Street, but it failed. Mr. Witherton was paid ten pounds this year for keeping school, and the following assignment of highways made:

"Isaac Chenery fhould mend the Rooad from bubling brook along by Nathl Gays coming Near John Halls and that Solomon Bullard fhould Take care and mend all the other Roads on the North fide of Spice brook, and that Ephraim Clark take care, & mend the Road beginning at Spice brook that brige and the Road Leading to Eafey plain and the Roads in Eafi Plain, and to James Smith beginning at the meeting houſe that Road Leading by Left Claps Leading up to Jonathan boydens and that road leading by Bardens and that Road leading by peter Fales."

This year the town again voted not to choose a Representative, giving the reason that they were not qualified.

At the March meeting of 1741, what is now the easterly part of East Street was extended as follows:

"Att the ſame meeting the Town Granted a Road from Dedham Line to Joseph Carrels land to a road which was formerly Laid out Beginning att Dedham Line at a oak stub the north ſide of ye Rhoad and to a White oak stub, and from thence to a Reid oake stand and to a White oake stand and from thence to a white oake Stand and from thence to Samuel Auſting and John Pettey to the Land of Joſeph Carrel where the Rhoad is all redy Laid out this Rhoad to be two roods wide whence Samuel Auſtin and Joseph pettey and John pettey Doe give the Land for ſaid Rhoad. This Rhoad Layd out by us the ſubſcribers.

"CAPT JOHN BOYDEN
"JOSEPH HARTSHORN
"LEUT JOSHUA CLAP."

At the meeting of May 19, 1741, the town was warned to choose for the county its first Register of Deeds. The names of Eleazer, and Benjamin Rhoads, afterwards well-known citizens of the east part of the town, first appear as citizens of the town.

We are pardoned for holding up our hands when we read that in 1742 that old meeting-house is still not quite finished, and that the reward for killing squirrels and blackbirds will fail to help the matter. The now pretty old house was still "going" to be finished two years later.

In 1744 Peter Lyon is described as the owner of a

grist-mill, and a milestone is noted on the way to the Plain "Near Robins paufter bares."

Seth Clap, Joshua Fisher, and the Widow Kingsbury taught school this year, the widow in her own house.

In 1745 there appears no reference to the Louisburg Expedition, joined by the Rev. Thomas Balch of South Dedham, but merely this remote entry to fishing:

"June ye 24, 1745 Affembled the Select men and ordered Ezekiel Robins to be our agent to make fearch and fe that there be a Convenient Sluice or pesage throu the pouder mill dam in Milton for the fish to pafs."

In 1746 deer reaves and town stocks were provided.

Aquilla Robbins and Mrs. Jeremiah Day taught in the schools this year. In 1748 Peter Lyon taught the children of the northeast part of the town and boarded at Robert Allen's.

This year Seth Kingsbury cared for the roads from Wrentham "line to the Sign of the Black horfe."

In 1748 Rachel Wilkinson, Mary Camp, and Rachel Fuller were warned out of town, and the warrant returned to the clerk of the Quarter Sessions.

In 1749 Deacon Robbins was granted the privilege of changing the stairs in the "weftly end of the meeting houfe and to build a Pew at his own Cost."

In 1749 the Selectmen warned out of "ye town William Marfhall and his wife and all his children."

In 1750 the name of Joseph Coney appears. This year the lands of Nathaniel Guild, Nathaniel Pribble, and others of Stoughton were joined to the town. In 1752

Ebenezer Bacon had charge of the school at the Centre. In 1753 the town warned out of its precincts the widow Deliverance Thompson, and the lands of Theodore Mann, Jedediah Morse, and James Plimpton were annexed.

"It was put to ye town whether they would accept of John Roads and Stephen Roads to be annexed to the Town of Walpole begining at the hornpine in trap hole brook and on sd Brook till it comes to ye Cuntry Road and upon ſd Road to the Southerly ſide of high Plain and it was voted in the Affirmitive. It was Put to the Town whether they would accept of Benjamin Roads William Wright Samuel Bradſhaw William Coney and Joſeph Wilkeſon Begining at the ſoutherly Part of ye Country Road upon high plain and from thence with a ſtraight Line to the North Eaſt Corner of Samuel Bradſhaws Land and from thence on the Cuntry Road till it comes to a way Leading to the Land of William Coney and from thence to the North Eaſt Corner of Col. Royals farme, and on ſd Royals till it comes to Blakes Land from thence a ſtraight Line till it comes to the North Eaſt Corner of Jedidiah Morſes Land and Round ſd Morſes Land till it comes to Plimpton weſterly bounds of his home Lot a ſtraight Line North weſt till it Comes to the Bound Line Between Walpole and Stoughton to be annexed to the Town of Walpole and it was Voted in the afermitive."

In 1753 the name of Jonathan Kendall, namesake of one of our streets, first appears.

"At the meeting of Nov. 2, 1753 it was voted to build one Pue over the Men's ſtairs and a Nother over the Womens ſtairs and a Nother at the foot of the Womens ſtairs and to ſhut up the Alley and Cloſe the Body of ſeats and it was Voted in the Afermitive."

In 1754 the minister, Rev. Phillips Payson, acted as school-teacher for the centre of the town. In this year Elnathan Boyden, known later as the ensign of Capt. Bacon's company, taught school in his father's house.

It was also voted to put another "tear of Gallerys in ye Meeting houſe."

Prices of articles of clothing of the day were given as follows: Ebenezer Clap was paid for a pair of shoes for Mary Lyon, who, with Peter Lyon, had fallen into straitened circumstances, 4 shillings, 8 pence, and Mary Fisher, for a "Pettecoat" for the same unfortunate, 8 shillings, and for a handkerchief 5 shillings.

The name of Spring or Beaverhole Brook is first used in 1755, and the following is given as the bounds between the town and the town of Stoughton:

"A stake and heap of ſtones at the Northermoſt branch of Trap hole Brook about four rods ſouth weſt from the horn bine tree and from thence to a heap of Stones not found ſuppoſed to be in Roadſes ſtone wall and from thence to a Maple ſtump with ſtones about it and from thence to a heap of ſtones and from thence to a ſtake and heap of ſtones by Deacon Fullers Path and from thence to a heap of ſtones by Ebenezer Fales Path to his saw mill on the east ſide of this Path and from thence to a heap of ſtones at the ſtump of a tree fallen and from thence to a Great white oak and from thence to a white oak in the Edge of a Swamp and from thence with a straight Line to Spice or Spring Brook and then a wet Line to ye Cuntry Road leading from Boston to Rhoad iland: and along ſaid Road to the ſouth Eaſt Corner of Nathl Guild Whome Lot to a heap of ſtones Between two Poſts Marked W.S. then the Line of the above ſd Guild as ſhown by him till it comes to a White oak marked; and from thence to a Poaſt and ſtones and from thence to a Large Red Oak and from thence to a ſmall Brook and upon ſd Brook, and that to be the Line till it comes to ſchool Meadow Brook and upon ſd Brook untill it comes to birds Lot and upon ſd Birds Lot weſterly untill it comes to the Northeaſt Corner of Enſn Theoadur mans Lot and then we find by ſundery acts of the General Court that the above ſd mans and James Plimpton, Jedidiah Morſe and allſo the

Eftate of Conl Royall of Charlftown Efqr his with their Eftates that Lay in ftoughton is annexed to the Town of Walpole."

In 1756 the town entered in its records the following:

"Walpole Febry ye 16, 1756 then asfembled ye Select Men and Granted out Warrant to warn Pricilla Day other wife Called Pricilla Nichols and Her Child called Mary Roads and Jeduthan Bullen to Depart out of this Town as the Law Directs."

This year Seth Kingsbury kept the Easy Plain school and Seth Clap kept the winter school at the Centre, and the successor of Joseph Carroll, Nicholas Harris, is first mentioned. Joshua Clap is allowed £2 9*s* 7*p* for "Providing ye Town ftock of Bullets & flint." An act of the town at the February, 1757, meeting to "grant money for ye Support of the Nutral French that ye General Court fent to this Town," for which £30 was afterwards granted, is worthy of mention, as also a payment to Capt. Joshua Clap for a half "Barrel of Pouder for ye Town stock," for the serious struggle between our settlements and the French and Indians was still going on.

A Mr. "Maafon" was the teacher in the east part of the town this year, and the minister's son, Swift Payson in the Centre.

The French refugees referred to were quartered at the old house of Jeremiah Dexter, near the old burying-ground, and the following persons were paid by the town in their behalf: Capt. Joshua Clap, Aquilla Robbins for firewood and other articles, James Clap for provisions, and John Hall for "corn and meet." Some did not survive their experience here, and, exiled and alone, found a too ready grave in the old near-by cemetery.

The youth having caused a good deal of unnecessary trouble in the meeting-house, the town this year "chose John Gregory, John Guild, Stephen Felch, Phillip Robbins and Nathaniel Pribble, to Infpect ye young People on ye Lords Days," and we can feel assured that, at least for the next Sunday or two, the inspection was pretty rigid.

The Overseers of the Poor, for the first time mentioned, are allowed £8 14*s* 10*p* for what they "Expended on the French that ye General Court afigned to this Town."

There is, also, a general sweeping and cleaning out. Ruth Farington, John Gould and his wife Hannah, Jedediah Thomas and Hannah, their three children, Peter Allen and his wife "and all their Children," John Mackewith and the widow Thorp, by order of the town had to emigrate to pastures fresh and new.

In 1758 the name of Dupee, once so well known on the Plain, occurs, when "Charles Duppe is paid three shillings & four Pence for Labour at ye Meeting houfe."

That the public may understand somewhat more clearly about our early school efforts, so misunderstood, it must read the following record:

"Walpole Feb. ye 14, 1758. Then afsembled ye Select Men and Granted out their warrant for a Town Meeting to be on March ye 7 at Nine o Clock in the Morning to except of a Prefent from ye Revd Mr. Payfon viz ye Land ye fchool houfe ftands upon: for the Town to except of a Prefent from Decon Robbins Viz the fchool houfe that he Built for ye Towns Ufe."

It is clear that any honor from the Town relating to naming our school buildings should first go to the more worthy man of the two. This is not the only grave mistake made by our school committee.

At the following March meeting

"The Town Excepted of the Prefent that ye Revd Mr Payfon Gave to this Town Viz ye Land that ye School houfe ftands on fo long as there fhall be a School houfe continued there. Ye Town excepted of ye Prefent that Decon Ezekiel Robbins Gave to ye Town viz ye School houfe that he Built for ye Town Ufe Viz fo many of ye Inhabitance as it will accomodate in the Place it Now ftands, and alfo the Land where the Pound is Now Built he freely gave to this Town fo Long as there is a Pound Continued there."

As far as naming the chief public structures in the Centre, it looks as though it should be the Payson as well as the Robbins Grammar School, as in the east part of the town the Allen or the Lewis name on one of its school buildings. The naming of public buildings should rest on undoubted long-established merit, and not left to either the ignorant newcomer or the weak toady. No one feels honored by the one or flattered by the other. Certainly the High School should have no other name than the Walpole High School.

At the town meeting Dec. 26, 1758, Seth Clap was granted five shillings and four pence for making a place in the meeting-house to secure the town stock of ammunition. There is no evidence that the place was in or even beneath the pulpit, as sometimes jocosely represented.

There is also something said about "Mr. Naafons

Petatar Yard" soon after this. It, for years after, served as a permanent bound in assignment of highways.

In 1760 the author's uncle, Seth Bullard, one of our first representatives to General Court, and captain of the Walpole company that marched on April 19, 1775, took the school in the east part of the town. Two years later Tabitha Robbins joined the small corps of school-teachers, and Samuel Rhoads, his wife, and all their children were warned out of town.

In 1762 a committee was chosen "to fill up Vacient feats & feat ye fore feats in ye upper Gallery in ye Meeting houfe." The town also voted that "ye fchool houfe that Deacon Robbins gave to this Town fo many as it will acomidate fhould be moved, Provided thofe that it will acomodate be at ye charge of Moveing it."

In 1763 our pastor's son, John Payson, and Mary Morse taught our schools. This year mention is made of the new doctors, Dr. Ebenezer Dagget, Dr. Fuller, and Dr. Locke. Nicholas Harris and Nathan Pond were constables. John Needham's name, so well known thereafter, is first mentioned, as of the Plain. £16 was granted this year for a "wreading and writing School to Be laid out by one Mafter in four Places in this Town, also £8 for a Women School."

In 1764, John Payson, Eleazer Jackson, Esther Boyden, Mary Morse and Tabitha Robbins also taught our schools. The highways were worked and repaired by "squadrens" at a daily wage of five shillings per man, and ten for man and team, and schools kept in houses of Deacon Fisher and Ezra Morse.

In 1765 Hephzibah Dexter, probably wife of Jeremiah Dexter, taught the Plain school.

There were made several attempts to choose a "Man to tune the Pfalm," but without success.

In 1767 Stoughtonham, afterwards Sharon, takes the place of Stoughton, as Stoughton had taken the place of Dorchester, as our easterly boundary.

In 1766 Mrs. Esther Hancock taught the Centre school, and Lydia Smith in the south part of the town, and in 1767 Ensign Mann, Doctor Daggett and Moses Fales were chosen to "Seat ye Lower Gallery Excepting ye fore Seat of ye frunt fo as to better accomidate ye Singing in ye Time of Publick Worfhip." Moses Fales and Joshua Clap, Jr., were also "Chosen to Tune ye Pfalm in ye Time of Publick Worfhip." The same year were ordered out of town Elizabeth Tinker and Mary Babcock.

In 1768 appear the following entries:

"To Eliphlet Ellis what he Paid Enoch Elifes wife for Schooling Laft Sumer 13*s* 11*p*. To Docr Daggett what ye Town Granted him for Doctring Ebenr Pettys wife £3 19*s* 11*p*. To Nicholas Harris for his Daughter keeping fchool by Willets laft fumer the fum of £3 4*s*."

There was a school at Ellis's corner the next winter. Benjamin Kingsbury, Sarah Harris, Hannah Partridge, and Lydia Mann, taught the same winter. There are many mentions of the exacting fines, so common at that period, all of which were devoted to the poor.

Under Sept. 19, 1768, appears this significant entry:

"Voted that they will Send one Perfon to Join the Committees at Faneail Hall."

Joshua Clap was chosen. Our first act of patriotism. In 1769 appears this item: "To Oliver Clap for his providing a Baize Gown for Ebenezer Pettee's wife, 13*s* 4*p*."

In 1770 Ebenezer Allen had charge of the Centre School, and John Hall was paid fifty cents a week for boarding Mrs. Petty, for years a town charge.

The mention is often made in the early records of Col. Royal's farm, and in 1770 appears the following:

> "Medford April ye 6, 1770 In Conformity to the province Law I am now to inform you that I have Let my Farm in Walpole (last in the Occupation of Mr. Michael Hatch) unto Mr Noah Edminfter and Mr Jofhua Hatch, the first is from Freetown has a Wife Named Louifa and five Children (viz) Two Sons and three Daughters. Mr Hatch was at Walpole before Introduced there by his Father he has a Wife and I think one Child. I Doubt not you will Caufe this my Intelligence to be noted in your Town Books. Am Gentleman your humble Servant
> "ISAAC ROYALL."

Nearly every warrant, since the incorporation of Walpole as a town, contained an article to see whether the town would choose a Representative, but it was always voted down, until May 24, 1770, when Joshua Clap, Esq., was elected to that office for that year.

In March, 1772, Aaron Blake and Nathan Pond were chosen of the selectmen, and Josiah Whittemore, who for years had repaired the glass in the meeting-house, and John Lewis of the highway surveyors.

In 1772 the minister of the town, for the first time, is offered a resting place while the congregation was tuning up. The town then "voted to Build a Seat in the Pulpit for the benefit of Mr. Payson if it is Defired." It is quite clear that this accommodation was offered solely on account of the minister's advanced age, and that ministerial laziness had little encouragement in those days.

This year Sarah Billings, wife of Jonathan Billings, taught school at Philip Barden's house, Mary Rhoades at the Centre, and Mary Sumner at the east part of the town.

It will be noticed that all references to the Indian have long ceased. A hundred years had passed since the father of Charles Josiah, our last Indian grantor, the powerful but vicious chief of our Indians here, during a seven years' war with the Mohawks of the West, had been slain, and his defeated braves driven back to our shelter at Punkapoag. With his son, their chief, under the guardianship of our governor, the tribe gradually relinquished war and roving for a quiet, uneventful and gradually decimating life alone by themselves.

CHAPTER VIII

NOT satisfied with the foregoing minute description of the town's activity in our early struggles with our enemies, some will ask for more explicit history. In 1754 the French and the allied Indians, with a claim of right, began to eagerly press in upon the borders of our little English settlements, all the way from Western Virginia, Pennsylvania, New York, to all of New England. The English government, the home government, alive to its danger and interests, sent over troops which were joined by our provincial volunteers, all under English officers. Then resulted the disastrous Braddock campaign in which George Washington served with such distinguished valor, the Oswego campaign of Governor Shirley, and the latter's Crown Point expedition.

In the latter were a large number of Walpole men, both in Capt. William Bacon's company, and in that of Capt. Eliphalet Fales. Both captains belonged in Dedham, the former having been one of the original members of the first South Dedham church. The following is the roster of the former's company, mustered in May 3, 1756, and belonging to Col. Richard Gridley's Regiment, with interesting description:

"Capt William Bacon, Dedham; Lieut. Ephraim Jackson, 27 years old, blacksmith, Roxbury; Ensign Elhanan Boyden, 25 years old, cooper, Walpole; Sergt. William Lewis, 32 years old, Dedham; Timothy Calahan, 22 years old, Dedham; Asa Semons, 18 years old, Dedham; Ephraim Gogin, 39 years old, Dedham; William Smith, 20 years old, blacksmith, Walpole; George Cleaveland, 45 years old, blacksmith, Walpole; Samuel Kindal, 21 years old, cordwainer, Walpole; William Marshall, 42 years old, weaver, Walpole; Jonathan Shepard, 25 years old, Bellingham; Thomas Ball, 37 years old, cordwainer, Walpole; Joseph Antony, 24 years old, Walpole; Nicholas Buckley, 29 years old, Walpole; John Woodcock, 24 years old, Dedham; William Grifis, 22 years old, mariner, Walpole; Thomas Balch, 18 years old, Dedham; John Smith, 20 years old, Walpole; Timothy Lewis, 18 years old, Dedham; Jonathan Boyden, 19 years old, Walpole; Ezra Bullard, 20 years old, Dedham; John Hooper, 19 years old, bloomer, Walpole; Joseph Morse, 25 years old, Dedham; Isaiah Lyon, 18 years old, miller, Walpole; James Weatherbee, 21 years old, Dedham; Adam Blackman, 20 years old, blacksmith, Walpole; Joseph Whittemore, 21 years old, Dedham; Ebenezer Boyden, 21 years old, Walpole; John Lewis, 18 years old, Dedham; Caleb Packard, 20 years old, Bridgewater; Joseph Lyon, 23 years old, Dedham; Daniel Leach, 20 years old, Bridgewater; Samuel Laughlin, 22 years old, Boston; Ebenezer Pratt, 18 years old, Bridgewater; Ezekiel Morry, 19 years old, Boston; Samuel Stacy, 21 years old, Taunton; Samuel Colburn, 22 years old, Boston; Philip White, 21 years old, Walpole; Hezekiah Weeks, 18 years old, Boston; Timothy Gay, 32 years old, Dedham; Moses Felt, 42 years old, Boston; Obediah Chandler, 19 years old, Boston; William Draper, 22 years old, Roxbury; William Ansis, 17 years old, Woburn; Nathaniel Blanchard, 21 years old, Roxbury; Timothy Draper, 20 years old, Dedham; David Dana, 21 years old, Brookline; Benjamin Ledoit, 29 years old, Dedham; John Richards, 30 years old, Roxbury; Joseph Lee, 22 years old, Dedham; David Fairbanks, 17 years old, Dedham; Edward Murfee, 50 years old, Roxbury; Henry Clemons, 42 years old, Dedham; Benjamin Clarke, 35 years old, Medfield; Ichabod Haley, 42 years old, Dedham; Benjamin King, 34 years old, Medfield; Benjamin Holden, 23 years old, Dedham; Hosea Abraham, Natick; John Lindsey, 23 years old, Dedham; Eleazer Thayer, 24 years old, Medway;

Joseph Ephraim, 22 years old, Dedham; William Larkin, 25 years old, Taunton."

Of these, Joseph Ephraim and Hosea Abraham were Indians, Edward Murfee and Timothy Calahan Irishmen.

Thomas Balch, who is called a laborer, was the son and namesake of Rev. Thomas Balch, the first minister of South Dedham. To his father's great sorrow he never lived to get home. So also Sergt. William Lewis. They both died near Stillwater, New York. The three Lewis men were first cousins, and are called volunteers in distinction from the hired men. Some of the men had served with Captain Bacon during the foregoing winter. They were all familiar with Indian warfare like the Lewis boys, for they were all mere boys less than twenty years of age, with the exception of William who was thirty-two. Eighty years before, their great-aunt Lydia Lewis McCloud with her husband and two children had been surprised outside of the stockade in Lancaster and tomahawked in cold blood. They had heard of John Monaco's bold assertion, "what me will me do." They had often been told of the vain efforts to Christianize and tame Indians generally. Perhaps they had heard them ask, as they sometimes did, "Does God understand Indian?" "Why does he not kill the Devil?" "What says a soul when it goes to heaven or hell?" "What do you get by praying? You go naked still and our corn is as good as yours," and felt their reformation hopeless. At home they belonged to Capt. Joseph Morse's company. Most of the Walpole men belonged to that of Capt. Oliver Clap.

The people here were beginning to take some interest

in outside matters. There were grievances they found, at least, after they had a Representative at General Court, and the following record should be carefully noted:

"Jany ye 12 1773 Voted that it is the opinion of this Town that our Rights and liberties are Infringed upon Which is a Great Grievance. Voted to Chufe a Committee of five men to prepare a Draft of Inftructions for our Reprefentative to be laid before the Town at the ajournment of this Meeting Chofe Enfn Seth Bullard, Mr Enoch Ellis Doctr Samuel Cheney Mr George Payfon Mr Aquila Robbins for Said Committee — then the Meeting was ajourned to fryday to meet again at 3 o'clock P M, the usual hour for town meeting.

"At an ajournment of a meeting of the freeholders and other Inhabitants of the Town of Walpole on the fifteenth Day of Jany, 1773, it was put to their Vote to accept of the Report of a Committee that was Chofen to Confider of publick Grievances and it paft in the Affirmative. Then Voted to have the above Report Recorded in the Town Records, then Voted to have a Coppy of fd Report tranfmitted to Joshua Clap Esq. our Representative, then voted to have a Coppy of fd Report tranfmetted to the Committee of Corrifpondance for the Town of Boston. Then the Meeting was Difolved.

"The Committee Appointed by the Inhabitants of the Town of Walpole the 12th of Jany 1773 to Confider of Publick Grievances report as follows:

"Firft we are Senfible that the Rights and Liberties of the People of the American Colonies are invaded and Infringed in many Inftances needles to be enumarated being Sufficiantly pointed out already by many in this province. Secondly we determine that we will unite with our Loyal Brethren in this and other Provinces in any Conftitutional manner as shall best appear to procure a Redrefs of our Grievances. Thirdly we Inftruct our Reprefentative to promote an Adrefs to his Majesty requefting him to repeal Such Acts as to us appear Grievous and that he the fd Representative ufe all pofible Precaution that faid Addrefs may Reach the Royal Ear. Fourthly, that our Reprefentative Enquire into a Report lately Spread Concerning the Dependancy of the Honourable Juftices of the Superior Court upon the Crown for Support and to act thereon as to him Shall seem Beft in order to prevent the evil thretened and likely therefrom to Enfue. Fifthly that if the Judges have not a Support from the Province adequate to their Important Stations and Services the Said Representative is hereby inftructed to ufe his Influence to procure the Same for them. Sixthly we Caution our Reprefentative a gainft being perfwaded of the friendly Intentions of any Perfon whatfoever who shall defignedly keep or endeaver to keep in Ignorance the People of the province refpecting the Salary of the Judges aforefaid.

"SETH BULLARD
"GEORGE PAYSON
"AQUILLA ROBBINS
"ENOCH ELLIS
"SAML CHENEY."

The following items are not very important, but perhaps will be a little suggestive to my readers:

"Feb ye 1st 1773 Afsembled the Selectmen and ordered Mr Benjamin Kingsbery Town Treafurer to pay to Jofhua Allen for making a Coffin for Robert Worfley *6s 8p* To Stephen Felch for Diging a Grave for Robbert Worfley *2s 8p*."

It was, a little later, also "voted to build a powder house six feet square and six feet between joints, and set it on the Widow Robbins' high hill if she consented to it."

Then follows more of that precious history of the Revolutionary struggle for Independence.

"Under June ye 30, 1774 the Town Voted to Grant the Sum of one Pound and four Shillings to be Paid to Mr Thomas Cushen Efqr in order to Enable a Committee of Congrefs (Chofen By the Jeneral Affembly of this Province) to meet with the Commitees of the other Provinces and Collonies in North Emericha. The Town mak Choice of Mr Seth Bullard an Agent to Deliver the Sum granted to the above Thomas Cufhen at Bofton and to take a Receipt for the same.

"The Town voted that they would act upon the Defire of the Committee of Correfpondance for the Town of Bofton Refpecting the importation of Goods from Great Briton. The Town chofe a Committee in order to Draw a form of a Covenant in order to be fubjoined unto. The Town Chofe Enoch Ellis Jofhua Clap Esqr Benjamin Kingsbery Seth Bullard Samuel Cheney, George Payfon & Theodore man a Committee.

"The Town Voted as an addition to the Town Stock of aminition one hundred and fifty Pound weight of Good Gun powder and Bullets and flints in Proportion as the Law Directs. The Town Chofe Dec. Samll Cheney to Provide the above Granted Amminition.

"Auguft ye 29, 1774 The Town Chofe three Deligats to meet the Committees of the other Towns in the County in order to Confult what meafures is Proper to be taken for the Safty of the Country. The Town made Choice of Mr Nath Guild Mr Enoch Ellis and Docrr Samuell Cheney as Delegats to Reprefent the Town at the County Convention to be held at Mr Woodwards at Dedham the Sixt Day of September Next and at other Conventions from time to time During the Towns Pleafure."

During this year Lois Gould and Judith Farrington were our school-teachers.

"Sept 26 1774 the Town Chofe a Committee to Give our Reprefentative Inftructions on Behalf of the Town the sd Committee Confisting of three Men (viz): Mr Nathl Guild, Capt Seth Kingfbery and Jofhua Clap Esqr. for the Purpofe above fd—(2) it was Voted that our Reprefentative Joyn in and with a Provincial Congrefs to be held where the Provincial Congrefs fhall apoint, and if the Cafe Should not admit that the fd Reprefentatives Could attend faid Congrefs the Town made Choice of Mr Nathl Guild to reprefent the Town at sd Congrefs.

"(3) the Town voted that they would Purchaf Two field Peices (4) the Town made choice of Mr Benjamin Kingfbery Capt Ebenezer Clap and Enfign Theodore man as a Committee in Behalfe of the Town to Purchas fd field Peices.

"Sept 30, 1774 (2ly) The Town voted to Choofe a Committee of

Correſpondence to Joyn with the Committees of other Towns in this Province Conſiſting of five men (Viz): Mr Nath Guild, Capt Seth Kingſbery, Enſn Theodore Man Capt Ebenezer Clap and Joſeph Day then this meeting was ajourned to ſuch time af the above ſd Committee shall apoint by aplying to the Town Clerk.

"The following Inſtructions for our Repreſentatives, as we have Choſen you to Repreſent us in the Great and General Court to be holden at Salem on Wedneſday the fifth Day of october Next Enſewing we Doe hereby Inſtruct you that in all your Doings as a member of the Houſe of Repreſentatives you adhere firmly to the Charter of this Province Granted by their Majesties King Willm and Queen Mary and that you Do no act that Can Poſibly be Conſtrued into an Acknowledgment of the Act of the Britiſh Parliment for Altering the Government of the Maſſachuſetts Bay. More Eſpecially, that you acknowledge the Honourable Board of Counſelers Elected by the General Court at their Seſſions in May Laſt (1774) as the only Rightfull and Conſtituſional Council of this Province; We Do hereby Inſtruct and Impower you to Join with the Members who may be Sent from this and the other Towns in this sd Province; and to meet with them at a time to be a Greed on in a Generall Provincial Congreſs to act upon Such matters as may concern you in ſuch a manner as may appear to you moſt Conducive to the true Intent of Intreſt of this Town, and Province and moſt likely to Preſerve the Liberties of all North America. In General the above Inſtructions were Voted at the ajournment of a meeting of the Inhabitants Sept ye 30, 1774."

This was followed by several adjournments and then appears the following:

"At a Meeting of the Inhabitants of the Town December ye 19, 1774 (on ajournment from the fifth Day of November 1774) it was Voted that they would Comply with the Method Prepoſed by the Provintial Congreſs for the more effectual Carrying into Execution the Aſſociation of the Continental Congreſs. (2) the Town Voted that they would Comply with what the Continental Congreſs Reſolved in 14 articles as they are ſpecifyed in the Publick Prints.

"(3) The Town Voted to Choose a Committee of Infpection Confifting of Seven Men (viz): Doctr Samll Cheney, Mr Enoch Ellis, Mr Nicholas Harris, Mr John Boyden Mr Phillip Robins Enfn Theodore Man and Mr Nathaniel Guild.

"(4) The Town Voted that they would Indemnify the Selectmen or Affeffors for Not making a Return of the Afseffment of the Provincial Rate to Harrifon Gray Esqr. (5) The Town Voted that they would Indemnify their Conftables in their Staying the Province Rate to Henry Gardner Efqr.

"At a meeting of the Town Decembr 30, 1774 By an ajournment of a meeting the fifth of November, the Town Voted to Send one Deligat to Reprefent the Town at a Provintial Congrefs, and Mr Enoch Ellis was Chofen for the above Purpofe.

"(2) it was Voted to Grant to Docr Samll Cheney the Sum of Twenty four Pounds for his Providing Amunition for the Town. Captt. Seth Bullard, Mr Aquilla Robbins, Mr George Payfon, Captt Jofeph Hartshorn; Mr Jofeph Day; Jofhua Clap jr. Captt Jeremiah Smith; Mr Aaron Blake, and Mr John Lewis were Chofen as an addition to the above Committee of Infpection and See how would Provid wood for the Suffering Induftrus Poor in the Town of Bofton."

On Dec. 30, 1774, the town voted:

"that one Quarter Part of the Traning Band Soldiars Should be Inlifted in the Province Service to be Ready at a minutes warning. (2ndly) the above fd minit men should be Paid out of the Town Treafury Two Shillings Pr Day for Each Day the above fd soldiars Shall be Called Together and shall be Exercized in the Military art or Difipline. (3ly) the Town Chofe Mr Willm Fifher, Esqr Clap and Capt Seth Kingfbery as a Committee To Say and Determine how often the above fd minit men Shall be called together to be Exercized and also to Determine how many hours fd men Shall Train in one Day; the above Committee to Vew the above fd Soldiars to fee whether they Bee able Boided men. 5ly the Town granted the fum of Twenty Pounds for the Encouragement of the above fd minit men to be Paid as above fd. 6ly the Town Voted that the Before Recited 14 Articles of the Refolves of the Contintial

Congrefs fhould be Recorded in the Town Book of Records by the Town Clerk."

This is followed by this interesting record, the orthography of which can easily be overlooked, like that of the preceding, in its importance in showing that our town early assumed the burden true patriotism always brings:

"At a meeting of the Town of Walpole December ye 19, 1774 By an ajournment of a meeting November ye 5th, 1774, it was Voted that the fourteen articles of the affociation of the Grand American Congrefs that met at Philidelpha the fifth of September Laft should be Entered on the Town Books as followeth:

"We his Majestys moft Loyal Subjects the Delegats of the Several Colonies of New hampshire, Maffachufetts Bay, Rhode Ifland, Coneticut, New York, New Jarfey, Penfylvania, the three Lower Counties of Newcaftel; Kent, Suffex, on Dellewere, Maryland, Virginia, North Carolina South Carolinia, Deputed to Reprefent them in a Continantl Congrefs held at Philadelphia on the fifth of September 1774 avowing our Ellegiance to his Magefty our affection and Regard for our fellow Subjects in Great Britan and elfewhere when affected with the Deepeft anxiety and moft alarming apprehentions at thofe Grievances and Diftreffes with which his Majefty's American Subjects are oppreffed, and having taken under our mouft ferious Deliberation, the State of the Whole Continent, find that the Prefent unhappy Situation of our affairs is occafioned by a Ruinous syftem of Colony adminiftration adopted by the Britifh Miniftry about the year 1763, evidently Calculated for Enflaving thefe Colonies, and with them the Britifh Empire in profecution of which Syftem, various Acts of Parliment have been Paffed for Raifing a revenue in America for Depriving the American Subjects in many inftances of the Conftitutional trial by Jury Expofing their Lives to Daingers by Directing an Illegal trial beyond the Seas for Crimes alledged to have been Commited in America; and in Profecution of the same Syftem, several Late Cruel and oppreffive acts have Been Paffed refpecting the Towns of Bofton and the Maffachufetts Bay, and alfo an Act for Extending the Province of Quebec fo af to border on the Weftern frontier of thefe Colonies. Eftablifhing an arbitrary Government therein a Difcouraging the Settlement of Britifh Subjects in that Wide and Extended Country thus by the Influence of Civil Principels and ancient Prejudices to Difpofe the Inhabitants to act with Hoftility againft the free Proteftant Colonies whenever a wicked Miniftry shall Chofe to Direct them. To obtain redrefs of thefe Grievances which Threaten Deftruction to the Lives Libertys and Property of his Majestys Subjects in North America, we are of opinion that a Non importation Nonconfumption and Non-exportation agreement faithfully adheared to will Prove the moft ready effectual and Peacable meafure, and therefore we Do for ourfelves and the Inhabitants of the Several Colonies whom we Reprefent firmly agree and affociate under the Sacred ties of Virtue, honour and Love of our Country as follows:

"(1ly) That from and after the firft Day of December Next we will not import into Britifh America from Great Britain or Ireland any Goods, Wears or merchandize as shall have Been exported from Great Britain or Ireland, nor will we After that Day import any Eaft India Tea from any Part of the world; nor any metalls, Syrups, Paneles, Coffee or Piementos from the Britifh Plantations or from Dominica, nor Wines from Madeira or the Weftern Iflands nor foreign Indigo.

"(2ly) That we will neither import nor Purchafe any Slaves imported after ye firft Day of December next after which Time we will wholy Difcontinue the Slave trade, and will Neither be Concerned in it ourfelves nor will we hire our Veffels, nor sell our Commodities or Manufactures to thofe that are Concerned in it.

"3ly) as a nonconfumption agreement Strictly adherred to will be an effectual Security for the obfervation of the non importation, we as above folemnly agree and affociate that from this Day we will not Purchafe or ufe any Tea imported on account of the Eaft India Company or any on which a Duty hath been or fhall be Paid; and from and after the firft Day of March next, we will not Purchafe or ufe any Eaft India tea whatever nor will we, nor fhall any Perfon for or under us Purchas, or ufe any Goods, wares, or merchandize we have agreed not to import, which we shall know or have Caufe to Sufpect, were imported after the firſt Day of December, Except ſuch as Come under the Rules and Directions of the tenth article hereafter mentioned.

"4ly) the Erneſt Deſire we have not to injure our fellow Subjects in Great Brition, Ireland or the weſt Indies induceſs us to Suſpend a non Exportation untill the tenth Day of September 1775; at which time if the sd acts and Parts of acts of the Britiſh Parliament herein after mentioned, are not Repealed, we will not Directly or indirectly export any merchandize or Commodity whatsoever, to Great Britain Ireland or the Weſt Indies except Rice to Europe.

"5ly) Such merchants as uſe the Britiſh Trade and Iriſh Trade, will Give orders as ſoon as Poſſible to their factors, agents and Correſpondents in Great Britain and Ireland not to ship any Goods to them, or any Produce whatſoever, as they cannot be Received in Amarica; and if any merchant reſiding in Great Britain or Ireland, Shall Directly or indirectly Ship any Goods, wares or merchandize for Amarica in order to Break the ſd non importation agreement or in any manner Controvene the Same on ſuch unworthy Conduct being well atteſted it ought to be made Publick and on the ſame Being ſo Done we will not from thenceforth have any Commercial Connection with such merchant.

"6ly) That such as are owners of Veſels Shall Give Poſitive orders to their Captain or maſters not to Receive on Bord their Veſels any Goods Prohibitted By the ſaid non-importation agreement upon Pain of immediate Diſmition from their Service.

"7ly) We will uſe our utmoſt Endeavours to improve the Breed of Sheep and Increas their Numbers to the Greateſt Extent, and to that end we will Kill them as Spairingly as may be eſpeciely thoſe of the moſt Profitable Kind nor will we Export any to the weſt Indies or elſe where, and thoſe of us who are or may become over Stocked with or can conveniently ſpare any Sheep will Diſpoſe of them to our Neighbours eſpecialy to the Gouverment.

"8ly) that we will in our Severall Relations encourage frugality œconomy and induſtry; and Promote agriculture, arts and manufactures of this Country, eſpecially that of Woole; and will Diſcountenance and Diſcourag every ſpecies of Extravagance and Diſſipation eſpecialy all horſe Racing and all Kinds of Gaiming, Cock fighting exhibitions of ſhewes, Plays and other Expenſive Diverſions and Entertainments, and on the Death of any Relation or friend None of us or any of our families, will go into any further mourning Dreſs than a Black Crape or Ribbon on the arm or hat for Gentlemen and a Black Ribbon and Neck lace for Ladies, and we will Diſcontinue the Giving of Gloves and Scarfs at funerals.

"9ly) That ſuch as are Venders of Goods, or merchandize will not take advantage of the Scarcity of Goods that may be occaſioned by the Aſſociation, but will sell the same at the Rate we have Been Reſpectively accuſtomed to do for Twelve months Laſt Paſt and if any Vender of Goods or Merchandize shall sell any Such Goods on higher terms or shall in any Manner, or by any Device whatſoever Violate or Depart from this Agreement, no Perſon ought nor will any of us Deal with any such Perſon, or his or her factor or agent at any time hereafter for any Commodity whatever.

"10ly) In Caſe any merchant, trader, or any other Perſon shall Import any Goods or Merchandize after the firſt Day of December, and before the firſt day of February next, the same ought fourthwith at the Election of the towns to be Either Re-ſhiped or Delivered up to the Committee of the County or town wherein they ſhall be Imported to be Stored at the riſque of the Importer untill the Non-importation agreement Shall Ceaſe; or be Sold under the Direction of the Committee aforeſaid, and in the Laſt mentioned Caſe the owner or owners of ſuch Goods Shall be reimburſed out of the Sales the firſt Coſt and Charges, the Profits, if any, to be applied towards relieving and imploying Such Poor Inhabitants of the Town of Boſton as are immediate sufferers by the Boſton Port Bill, and a Perticular account of all Goods so Returned, Stored or Sold to be inſarted in the Public Papers; and if any Goods or Merchandize ſhall be imported after the ſaid firſt Day of February Next the Same Ought forthwith to be Sent Back again, without Breaking any of the Packings thereof.

"11ly) that a Committee be Choſen in every County, City and Town by thoſe who are Qualified to Vote for Repreſentative in the Legiſlature whoſe Buiſineſs it Shall be attentively to obſerve the Conduct of all Perſons touching the Aſſociation and when it shall be made to appear to the Satiffaction of a Majority of any Such Committee that any Perfon within the Limits of their appointment hath Violated this affociation that Such Majority forthwith Caufe the Truth of the Cafe to be Publifhed in the Gazetee, to the End that as Such foes to the Rights of Britifh America may be Publickly known, and univerfally Contemned as the Enemies of American Liberty and thenceforth we Refpectively, will break off all Dealings with him and her.

"12ly) that the Committee of Correfpondance in the Refpective Colonies Do frequently infpect the Cuftom houfes and Inform each other from time to time of the true State thereof, and of every other Material Circumftance that may occurr relative to this affociation.

"13ly) That all Manufactures of this Country be Sold at Reafonable Prices, that no undue advantage be taken of a future Scarcity of Goods.

"14ly) and we do further agree and Refolve that we will have no Trade Commerce, Dealings or Intercourfe whatfoever with any Colony or Province in North America which shall Exceed to, or which Shall hereafter Violate this affociation. But will hold them as unworthy of the rights of freedom and as inimical to the Liberties of their Country. And we Do Solemnly bind our felves and our Conftituents under the ties aforefaid to adheer to this affociation, untill Such Parts of the Several Acts of Parliament Paffed Since the Clofe of the Laft war, as impoft or Continual duties on Tea, wine, Molaffes, Syrups, Paneles, Coffee, Sugar, Piemento, Indigo, foreign Paper, Glafs, and Painters Colours, imported into America, and extend the Powers of Admiralty Courts beyond their ancient limits. Deprive the American Subject of trial by jury, authorize the Judges Certificate to Indemnify the Profecutor from Damages, That he might otherwife be Liable to from trial by his Peers, Require oppreffive Security from a Claimant of Ships or Goods Seized before he shall be allowed to Defend his Property, are Repealed and untill that Part of the Act of the 12G. 3, Chap 24, entitled 'An Act for the Better Securing his Majeftys Dock yards, Magazines, Ships, Ammunition, and Stores, by which any Perfonf Charged with Committing any of the offences therein Defcribed in America may be tried in any Shire or County within the Realm, is Repealed, and untill the four Acts Paffed in the Laft feffion of Parliment, Viz: that for Stopping the Port and Blocking up the harbor of Bofton. That for altering the Charter and Goverment of the Maffachufetts Bay. And that which is entitled 'An Act for the Better adminiftration of Juftice &c.' and that 'for extending the Limits of Quebec &c,' are Repealed, and we Recommend it to the Provintial Conventions and to the Committees in the Refpective Colonies to Eftablifh such further Regulations as they may think Proper for Carrying into Execution this Affociation. The foregoing Affociation being Determined upon by the Congrefs was ordered to be Subfcribed by the Several members thereof and thereupon we have hereunto set our Refpective names accordingly. In Congrefs Philadelphia October 20, 1774. Signed Peyton Randolph, Prefident. For New Hampfhire John Sulivan, Nath Folfom. Maffachufetts Bay: Thomas Cufhing, Samll Adams, John Adams, Robert Treat Pain. Rhode Island: Stephen Hopkins, Samll Ward. Connecticut: Eliphalet Dyer, Roger Sherman, Silas Deane. New York: Ifaac Low, John Alfop, John Jay, James Duane, Willm Floyd, Henrey Wifner, S Boerum. New Jersey: James Kinfly, Wm Livingfton, Stephen Crane, Richard Smith. Pennfylvania: Joseph Galloway, John Dickinfon, Charles Humphreys, Thomas Miflin, Edward Biddle, John Morton, George Rofs. New Caftle &c: Cæsar Rodney, Thomas McKean, George Rodgers. Virginia: Richard Henrey Lee, George Wafhington, P Henry Jun, Richard Bland, Benjamin Harrifor, Edmond Pendleton. North Carolina: Willm Hooper, Jofeph Hewes, R. Cafwell. South Carolina: Henry Middleton, Thomas Lynch, Chriftopher Gadfen, John Rutledge, Committee."

At the March meeting, 1775, John Lewis was chosen constable, and Isaac Lewis, Isaac Smith, and Aaron Clap sworn into office. Isaac Lewis and Richard Hartshorn were highway surveyors also in 1776.

Several town meetings were held before and after the Battle of Concord and Lexington, but no mention is made of any unusual anxiety, although Capt. Seth Bullard had led his company of Walpole men in the six days' service there; but at the first meeting after that memorable event the record runs thus:

"May ye 10, 1775 Then Afsembled the Select men and ordered Mr Benjamin Kingfbery Town Treafurer or Succefsor to Pay the Several Perfons hereafter Named the Several Sums annexed to their Names as followeth:

"to Levi Lindley a minute man the fum of 0 14 0 in full.
"to John Laurance a minute man the fum of 0 06 0 in Part.
"to Elias Man a minute man the fum of 0 06 0 in Part.
"to Peter Lyon a minute man the fum of 0 14 0 in full.
"to Daniel Morfe a minute man the fum of 0 14 0 in full.
"to Jeremiah Smith a minute man the fum of 0 12 0 in full.
"to James Fales Jr a minute man the fum of 0 13 0 in full.
"to Benjamin Carrell a minute man the fum of 0 12 0 in full.
"to Andrew Willett a minute man the fum of 0 14 0 in full."

In June Enoch Ellis received 14*s* for his service on the same occasion. There were many others still unpaid. James Clap received 14*s* for seven days' training; David Farrington 12*s*. June 2, 1775, Enoch Ellis was chosen delegate to represent the town at the "Congress to be held at Waterton for Six months next Enfuing."

This is followed by another grant for the urgent military service impending.

"At a Meeting of the 2nd of June 1775 the Town Voted to Raife fifty men as minute men and the Town granted four Shillings per Day for their Incoragement, and at a meeting on the tenth Day of July 1775 the Town Negatived the above sd vote and fo concluded not to Put any men under Pay more than were Lifted already."

This can only be explained by the fact that already a

large number were in service. Capt. Seth Bullard, with his Walpole company, at least, was in service, as appears from the following:

"At a meeting of the Town of Walpole Leagally Affembled at the Meeting houfe July 10, 1775 the Town made Choice of Mr Benjamin Kingsbery to Reprefent the Town at the Great and General Court to be held at Watertown, the twentyith firft Day of this Inftant July, and at two o'clock the 3d Day the Towne made Choice of Deacon Benjn Kingsbery for a Select man in the Room of Captt Seth Bullard now in the Army at Roxberry. The Town made choice of Captt Jofeph Hartfhorn for a Committee man of Correfpond in the Room of Coll. Ebenezer Clap now in the army."

Several payments for "bullet bags" now appear, an item of a "winding sheet," and one showing the term of Representative usually lasted 106 days.

At the March meeting of 1776, among the selectmen chosen were "Col. Seth Kingsbury, Major Seth Bullard," and "Capt. Jeremiah Smith," showing promotion for their late military service. As a Committee of Correspondence, Inspection, and Safety, Capt. Joseph Hartshorn, Enoch Ellis, Lieut. John Boyden, Nicholas Harris, and Nathan Kingsbury were chosen. Jacob Clap, Benj. Boyden, Henry Smith, Jr., Jacob Gay, Isaac Lewis, and Richard Hartshorn were chosen surveyors of highways, Joshua Allen tithingman, and Samuel Copp and Abel Allen field drivers. In the April following the town voted to use its efforts to have a registry of deeds and judge of probate in every town.

The names of Capt. Seth Bullard's Walpole Company, serving on the march to Concord and Lexington, are as follows. (It should be remembered that out of a population of less than eight hundred, we sent one hundred and fifty-seven men, who, on the beat of the alarm drum on that glorious morning, followed Seth Bullard over the fields to Concord. Their course was through Medfield, Dover, and Sherborn. Two companies, with twenty-five who joined a Medfield Company, formed our patriotic contribution to that noble beginning of our struggle for independence.)

A Muster Roll of a Militia Company in Walpole in Coll John Smiths Regt. marched in consequence of the alarm Apr. 19 1775

Seth Bullard, Capt., Elipht Ellis, Lieut, Enoch Ellis, Enfign, Samuel Smith, Sergt., Thomas Ritter, Sergt., Henry Partridge, Sergt., Eben Gay, Corp., Nathaniel Nason, Corp., Ebenezer Hartfhorn, Corp., Aaron Clark Fales, Fifer, Jotham Morse, Eleazer Partridge, Ezekiel Boyden, Benoni Morse, John Ellis, Moses Ellis, Jacob Kingsbery, Seth Kingsbery, John Boyden, Richard Hartshorn, Henry Smith, Jr., Solomon Kingsbery, Asa Ellis, Jacob Gould, Calvin Gay, Jabez Boyden, John Hartshorn, Bezalel Turner, Ziba Baker, Ebenezer Day, Samuel Thompson, James Clap, Jacob Clap, Elisha Hall, Eliphalet Ellis, Joseph Boyden, Samuel Guild, Joseph Guild, Ebenezer Farrington, William Pettee, Josiah Whittemore, Obadiah Morse, Nathaniel Gay, Benjamin Kingsbery, Ebenezer Fales, John Gregory, John Lewis, Abner Turner, Nicholas Harris, Joseph Kingsbury, Samuel Boyden, Ebenezer Farrington, Jr, Thomas Howard, Josiah Hall, Seth Hart, Elihu Lawrence, Moses Chamberlain, Asa Kingsbery, Isaiah Lyon, Amos Ramsdale, Samuel Rhodes, Joshua Hews, John Day, John Boyden, Samuel Cheney, George Payson, Seth Payson.

The twenty-five Walpole men in Capt. Sabin Mann's Medfield Company were Joshua Clap, Lieutenant, William Bacon, Ensign, Benjamin Carroll, Benjamin Pettee, Jeremiah Boyden, Jeremiah Smith, Ichabod Reed, Samuel Hartshorn, Elias Mann, James Fales, Willabor Nason, Amos Turner, Seth Clap, Samuel Fuller, Joshua Clap, 3d, David Farrington, James Smith, David Morse, Peter Lyon, Abel Baker, Abiel Pettey, Stephen Fuller, Joseph Day, John Laurence, Stephen Dexter. This one hundred and fifty-seven men must have taken nearly all the able-bodied men in town.

A MUSTER ROLL OF CAPT. JEREMIAH SMITH CO. IN COLONEYS SERVICE WHICH MARCHED FROM WALPOLE, DEC. 4, 1775, IN COL. JOHN SMITHS REGIMENT

WALPOLE, December ye 4, 1775

Jeremiah Smith, Capt. Philip Robbins, Lieut., John Boyden, 2rd Lieut., Oliver Clap, Sergt., Benjamin Hartshorn, Sergt., Ebenezer Fales, Sergt., Abel Allen, Sergt., Jeremiah Fales, Corp., Elijah Plympton, Corp., Ichabod Clap, Corp., Aaron Fales, Fifer, Timothy Man, Joseph Ellis, Jonathan Boyden, Jeremiah Blake, Asa Page, Joshua Allen, Samuel Copp, Joseph Tucker, Aaron Morse, Aaron Blake, Joseph Fales, Eliphalet Fales, Edward Cleaveland, Joshua Boyden, Timothy Cudwerth, George Cleaveland, Matthias Puffer, Samuel Allen, Charles Page, Moses Fales, Benjamin Man, Joseph Carroll, Jr., Nathaniel Guild, Jr., Fisher Hartshorn, Ebenezer Page, Joseph Page, Thomas Nason, Elijah Clap, Asa Plimpton, Jonathan Carrill, Christopher Smith, Timothy Hartshorn, John Dexter, Jonathan Kindall, John Cleaveland, Thomas Page, Eliphalet Clap, Moses Fales, Jr., John Frizzel, Elijah Lyon, David Boyden, Jeremiah Dexter, Thedore Man, Asa Fisher, Abiather Fales, Jonathan Boyden, Jr., Abner Guild, Ebenezer Clap Jr., Eleazer Clap, Aaron Farrington, Philip Bardens, Jr., Joseph Man, Jonathan Dexter.

Capt. Aaron Guild, later in the Revolutionary War, with a company of Walpole men, helped to construct

Washington's Dorchester Heights' entrenchments, which so completely commanded the British-ridden town of Boston, that it was evacuated by the enemy without delay.

Capt. Clap, also, led a company of Walpole in defence of our coast at Warwick, Rhode Island. Besides these, many continued to join the ranks of our struggling army, and it would be interesting to read of their varied experiences.

An artillery man from Walpole who served under General Washington when he crossed the Delaware, and later at the battle of Monmouth, where Moll Pitcher, after the fall of her husband, seized his swab and continued to serve his field-piece to the end of that hotly contested engagement, was reported to have grasped a cannon which had been dismounted, and so hot that it burnt through to his very flesh, and unaided, amid the wild cheers of his smoke-begrimed comrades, set it in position again and continued firing.

This epoch of our Revolutionary history, which seems to us so full of glory and success, was a far different matter to our forefathers. Poverty, sickness, ruin, and death were common attendants at every fireside. Even until the breaking out of the 1812 war there was hardly a reprieve.

"A MUSTER ROLL OF CAPT. OLIVER CLAP'S COMPANY, COL. WHEELOCK REGT., ON ALARM DEC. 8, 1776 AT WARWICK, R. I.

Capt. Oliver Clap, Lieut. Ebener Fales, Serg. Asa Fisher, Serg. David Cleaveland, Corp. Benjamin Hawes, Corp. Samuel Copp, Abiathar Fales, Samuel Allen, Joshua Allen, Abel Allen, Jonathan Boyden, John Boyden, Eliphalet Clapp, Seth Clapp, Jr., Jacob Clap, Joseph Ellis, Asa Ellis, Jonathan Fales, Joseph Fales, Nathaniel Guild, Amos

Morse, Joseph Man, Thomas Page, Charles Page, Asa Plympton, John Smith, John Smith, Jr., Eliphalet Smith, Joseph Tucker, Abner Gould.

VOL. III, P. 16, PAY ROLL CAPT. TIMOTHY MAN'S CO. ALARM JULY 17, 1780, RHODE ISD.

Timothy Mann, Capt., Benjamin Pettee, Lieut., Richard Hartshorn, Serg., Joseph Carroll, Serg., Asa Kingsbury, Sergt., Eliphalet Ellis, Sergt., Jacob Kingsbury, Corp., Joseph Mann, Corp., Abiathar Fales, Corp., John Smith, Corp., Joseph Page, Phineas Boyden, Aaron Blake, Elijah Boyden, William Bacon, Thaddeus Clap, Asa Clap, David Day, Joseph Ellis, Daniel Farrington, Calvin Gay, Alpheus Lyon, Libeus Page, Daniel Robbins, Oliver Smith, Riol Smith, Samuel Smith, George Talbott, Billing Clap, Asa Fisher, Joseph Boyden, Eliphalet Clap, Amos Kingsbury, Moses Smith, Joseph Turner, Samuel Allen, William Clap, William Marshall, John Marshall, Otis Partridge, Christian Smith, Nathan Turner, Nathaniel Bradshaw, Benjamin Hartshorn.

WALPOLE MEN 6 MOS MEN, 1780.

Levi Lindley, Joseph, Jackson, Joseph Pitchin, Daniel Morse, John Neal, Ebenr Farrington, John Merriam, Eliphalet Clapp, Abner Gould, Aquilla Cheney, Elisha Lawrence, David Turner, Charles Stebehen, James Stebehen, Nathan Pond, Benjamin Pettee, Samuel Hartshorn, Jesse Hartshorn.

The records go on, "May ye 10, 1776, it was voted that the Selectmen take particular care that the Burying Place be not fed." At this time every section of the town had its school, the centre, east and south receiving about £6, the north £5 10*s*, and the west £2 3*s*, of the school money.

The town also voted "to agree with Dr. Gerald about setting up Innoculation for the Small Pox at the houſe of Micah Baker, and made choice of Mrſs. Geo. Payson & John Lewis to set in the upar Gallery in ye Meeting houſe to prevent ye Children playing at meeting." It was also voted, and here for the first time dollars are mentioned, "that 50 Dollars should be reconed a whole term for the prefent Campain at Canady"; also "voted that Majr. Bullard should take the money which was fubfcribed to raife men, and hire men therewith if Opportunity should Offer at 50 Dollars per Man."

At the October meeting, at which Major Seth Bullard presided, appears the following most important and interesting action for a State Constitution:

"2ly Voted that the prefent Houfe of Reprefentatives of this State, together with the Council, if they confent in one Body with the Houfe, and by equal Voice should Confult & agree on such a Conftitution & form of Government for their state as the fd Houfe of Reprefentitives & Council as aforefaid on the fulleft and moft mature Deliberation shall Judge will moft conduce to the Safty, Peace & Happinefs of this State Provided they will direct that the same be made Publick for the Inspection and Perufal of said Town before the Ratification thereof by said Afsembly."

Every Walpole man should appreciate this early, wise and worthy declaration of political principle.

Immediately following appears this:

"Voted to chufe a Committee confifting of 5 Perfons to Examine what every one has done in the Town in the War. And Major Bullard, Mr Nathan Guild, Benj Kingsbury, Mr Enoch Ellis and Capt. Jeremiah Smith were chofen."

Under Nov. 4, 1776, appears "to Mr. Jacob Mann for keeping school," "to Mr. Enoch Ellis for his wives keeping school, and alfo to pay to Mr. Jona Boyden the sum of three shillings & eight pence for Helving 14 Axes for the Ufe of this State."

In 1777 it was "voted that the Men that served the Continent & State at Roxbury & the Places adjacent should be allowed 13 shillings & 4 pence per month & that the men that served at N. York & Ticonderoga should be allowed 3 Pounds per month — that the men that went to Warwick should be allowed 13 shillings & 4 Pence per month."

It becoming almost impossible to procure soldiers, the town raised its offer as follows: "Voted to give 14 Pounds in addition to what the Congrefs and General Court had granted to who should Inlift before ye 1st of March, 1777." The town had to borrow this bounty money.

At the March meeting in 1777 it was "Voted that there be granted 13 6 8 pr Year to Each able Bodied affective Soldiar that shall Inlift into the Continental Service for three years (viz.), 13 6 8 at the Time of his Pafsing mufter for the town of Walpole; and the Like Sum of 13 6 8 at the Entring of the Second year; and 13 6 8 at the Entring of the Third Year. Provided that fd Soldiar be in Immediate Service at Each term Before mentioned; Provided that fd Soldiar shall Inlift within one month from this 17th Day of March Inftant." In May of the same year a committee was chosen to "Notify the South Part of the Mail Inhabitants of this Town to meet at the Meeting Houfe the 15th Day of this Inftant May at eight o'clock in the forenoon Compleat with arms fite for Viewing." Deacon Benjamin Kingsbury was chosen to "Reprefent the Town in the Great and General Court this year."

June 16, 1777, the town voted to purchase a brass field piece, four-pounder.

In September, 1777, the town voted to unite the two Walpole militia companies into one, with Oliver Clap Captain, Timothy Mann First Lieutenant, Andrew Willett Second Lieutenant.

In March, 1778, the town voted to grant £5000 to be assessed on the polls and estates to carry on the war.

In June, 1778, the following resolve was passed: "Voted to return the thanks of the town to the revnd Ministers that Carried on the Publick services of our Late faſt, for their Good and kind Labours of love & to apply to them for advice Concerning the reſettlement of the Goſpel amongſt us."

In November, 1778, "Madam Payson was allowed £10 for providing for their minister on Sabbath, when the pulpit was supplied," and £4 10*s* to her stepson, George Payson, for boarding the minister at the town fast. And Jeremiah Blake is allowed £15 "for one Quarter of a Continental man." On Nov 27, 1778, £46 13*s* 3*p* was allowed the Rev. Mr. Bullard and Rev. Mr. Daniels for preaching. The town's old pastor, the Rev. Phillips Payson, had died the preceding January.

At the meeting May 20, 1779, Major Seth Bullard was chosen Representative to General Court.

June 24, 1779: "Voted to Give a Soldier that shall engage for nine months, one Thousand Dollars or otherwiſe pay them at the Rate of forty shillings per Month in the Produce of the Land, Rye at 4*s* per Buſhel, Indian Corn at 3*s* 4*p* per Buſhel. Beef at 2½*s* per lb., freſh

Pork at 3½s pr lb Butter at 8p pr lb, and other Eateables Equivalent."

In July, 1779, Lieut. William Bacon and John Lewis were chosen tax collectors. On November, 1779, it was voted to have no other candidate for the vacant pulpit but Mr. Read, and to prepare for building a new meeting-house.

In April, 1780, it was voted to pay "Soldiers to Carry on the war, £6000," for that year. The Continental currency had depreciated to this alarming extent.

In June thirteen more men were raised for the Continental Army, and the following vote was passed:

"Voted to Give the Soldiers that we agreed with to Join the Continental Army for Six months one Thoufand Dollars immediately upon their pafsing Mufter to each one of them and half a Bufhel of corn Pr Day from the Day they pafs Mufter till they are Difcharged, and after that time, half a Bufhel of Corn for every twenty Miles travel home, and Said men to be freed from their Poll Tax while in the Service. Said men to be paid in Corn or the Value thereof in Money if they se Caufe."

On Sept. 4, 1780, is given the following most interesting record, the first mention of the vote for a Governor:

"Made Choice of John Hancock Esqr for Governor by 35 votes.

"Voted for James Bowdoin Esqr. for Lieut Governor by 6 votes.

"Voted for Thomas Cufhen Esqr for Lieut Governor by 4 votes.

"Voted for Caleb Davis for Lieut by 1 vote.

"Senators, for Esqr Niles, 13 votes, Boston; Oliver Wendall, 13 votes Boston; John Pitts, 13 votes, Boston; Esqr White, Brookline; Increase Sumner, 13 votes, Roxbury; Deacon Fisher, 11 votes, Franklin."

To show the alarming depreciation of our currency, the following vote must be studied:

"Jany ye 4, 1781 Voted to Inftruct the Afsefsers to afsefs the Town for Eight Hundred Bufhels of Indian Corn at Sixty Dollars Pr Bufhel to pay the three months Men. Granted that one Thoufand Silver Dollars be forthwith afsefsed on this Town to hire Continental Soldiers."

Few people know that Medfield was ever wanted for our shire town.

At the same meeting it was

"Voted that this town will Concur with the Acts of the Convention with Refpect to Dividing the County, provided the Towns Round Join So as to make Medfield the shire Town."

At this meeting the following action was taken on the proposed new meeting-house:

"Voted to Build a meeting house agreeable to a plan that was Drawn of Manffield Meeting Houfe, and that all Pewes be Sold to the Highest Bidder one on each side of the Pulpit wall Pews.

It soon became necessary to hire soldiers for a longer term. The end of the war seemed still far away.

"Voted that the Committee for hiring the Continental men for three years or During the war Stand and Exert themfelves. Voted to Give the three years men Eighty hard Dollars on their Entring and Eighty hard Dollars a year During their Service, the first Eighty Dollars to be Recond for one year."

At this time Asa Ellis was paid "for Doing a tower in the War, 1555 Dollars," "William Fisher $500, Samuel Fuller $315, John Cleveland $600, John Lewis $600, and Nicholas Harris $600." Two French soldiers received £2206. Jonathan Kendall was paid £461 for "keeping minifters Horse." Fifty dollars per day was paid the soldiers going to Tiverton, and a horse cart was also provided to carry their packs to Slade's Ferry.

There are many interesting lists in the records, such as private contributions to aid the soldiers and for their monthly payments. The following public list is typical:

"December ye 20, 1781 afsembled the Selectmen and ordered Mr Nathan Pond, Treafurer to pay to the several Perfons the several Sums following for Cloathing they found for the Army, to Nathan Pond for 2 Blankets and 6 Shirts £6, to James Clap 6 shirts £3 12*s*, to Bezaliel Turner 5 pair stockings, £1 15*s*, to William Pettee 6 pairs of Shoes £3, to Ephraim Clark 2 pair of Shoes & one shirt £1 12*s*, to Ebenr. Baker 1 pair Stockings 7*s* to Henry Smith 2 pairs stockings 14*s*, to Jonathan Carrell 2 pair Shoes & 2 pair Stockings £1 14*s*, to Capt Man 1 pair shoes 10*s*, to Benj. Boyden 1 Shirt & 1 pair Stockings 19*s*, to Afa Smith 2 Shirts & 1 Blanket £2 8*s*, to Benj Pettee 6 pair Shoes (he was a shoemaker), 1 pair of stockings & 1 Blanket £4 11*s*, Madam Payson (the ministers widow) 1 pair Stockings 1*s*, Deacon Kingsbury 2 pair shoes £1, James Dupee 4 Blankets £4 16*s*, Lydia Boyce 2 Shirts & 3 pair Stockings £2 5*s*."

There is also a long list of those who advanced money to hire soldiers, of whom Elisha Hall lent $50, Nathan Pond $300, Joshua Allen $100, James Dupee $200, Capt. Oliver Clap $300, Ebenezer Fales $200, Samuel Thompson $100, Timothy Hartshorn $200, Capt. Jeremiah Smith $410, Capt. John Boyden $200, Benjamin Morse $120, Joseph Day $450, Major Seth Bullard £151 2*s*, Deacon Kingsbury $100, Col. Seth Kingsbury £156 2*s*, Nathaniel Bradfhaw $60, Stephen Dexter $100, Isaac Lewis $200, Josiah Hall $40, Jacob Clap $200, Oliver Ellis $40, Benj. Pettee $200, George Payson $200, Daniel Fisher $600, Abel Allen $200, Doct. Seth Man $50,

Aaron Blake $400, Samuel Guild $100, Calvin Gay $120, Richard Hartshorn $300, Capt. Shubael Downs $1000, Benjamin Kingsbury $200, Samuel Allen $78, William Robbins $200, Jonathan Boyden $200, Nathaniel Guild $225, Asa Fisher $300, John Lewis $300, Col. Ebenr Clap $200.

A Muster Roll of the Company under the command of Capt. Seth Bullard in Col. Joseph Reads Regt., to the last of Aug. 1775, 3 mos men.

Seth Bullard, Capt., Walpole
Thomas Pette, 1st Lieut., Walpole
Ezekiel Plimpton, 2d Lieut., Medfield
Levi Lindley, Serj., Walpole
Asa Fisher, Serj., Walpole
Eliphalet Fales, Serj., Dedham
Joseph Plimpton, Serj., Medfield
Samuel Boyden, Corp., Walpole
Eliphalet Fisher, Corp., Medfield
Elias Mann, Corp., Walpole
Ichabod Reed, Corp., Walpole
Abiather Fales, Drummer, Walpole
David Ellis, Fifer, Walpole
Anthony Bracket, Private, Walpole
George Blen, Private, Walpole
Philip Bardens, Private, Walpole
Nathan Baker, Private, Medfield
Nathan Bullard, Private, Medfield
Joseph Cole, Private, Medfield
Moses Chamberlain, Private, Walpole
Benjamin Carril, Private, Walpole
Ebenezer Clap, Private, Walpole
Eleazer Clap, Private, Walpole
Rufus Clark, Private, Medfield

Jabez Clark, Private, Medfield
Jonathan Dexter, Private, Walpole
William Everett, Private, Dedham
Jacob Ellis, Private, Walpole
Benjamin Fisher, Private, Dedham
John Fuller, Private, Medfield
James Fales, Private, Walpole
David Farrington, Private, Walpole
Aaron Farrington, Private, Walpole
Matthias Armsby, Private, Medfield
Jonathan Boyden, Private, Walpole
Ebenezer Farrington, Private, Walpole
Abner Gould, Private, Walpole
Joshua Hewes, Private, Medfield
Josiah Hall, Private, Walpole
Seth Hart, Private, Walpole
Asa Kingsbury, Private, Walpole
Cornelius Kollock, Private, Medfield
John Lawrance, Private, Walpole
Elihu Lawrance, Private, Walpole
Peter Lyon, Private, Walpole
Isaiah Lyon, Private, Walpole
Ebenezer Lyon, Private, Medfield
Ebenezer Merriam, Private, Walpole
_______ Mann, Private, Dedham
Abner Morse, Private, Walpole
Nathaniel Nason, Private, Walpole
Joseph Mann, Private, Walpole
Moses Peters, Private, Medfield
Abiel Pettee, Private, Walpole
Amos Ramsdale, Private, Walpole
Jonathan Read, Private, Attleborough
Samuel Rhoads, Private, Walpole
Jeremiah Smith, Private, Walpole
James Smith, Private, Walpole

Thomas Trott, Private, Medfield
Holland Wood, Private, Medfield
——— Wood, Private, Medfield
Jonas White, Private, Dedham
Andrew Willett, Private, Walpole

Mary Lewis taught one of the schools in 1782, 11 weeks, £3 17s; and Anne Neales, 12 weeks, £2 3s 2p; Margaret Man, 8 weeks, £2 16s; Rhoda Fairbanks, 12 weeks, £2 14s.

Nov. 18, 1782, it was voted to "build a new meeting house on the place where the old one now stands." The town soon purchased of Jacob and Ichabod Clap an enlargement of the meeting-house common, thus enabling a final removal of the church farther south, as indicated in the two plans of Walpole filed in the State House in 1831. The meeting-house there indicated is almost in front of the present apothecary shop.

During the Revolutionary period, the town carried its part of the burden with proper manliness, supporting both the soldier and his family. In 1780 measures were taken to procure its share of corned beef for the suffering army and necessaries for the soldier's families.

In 1782 the vacancy made by the death of the Rev. Phillips Payson was still unfilled, and at the March meeting appears the following record: "To fee if the Town will concur with the church in giving Mr. Porter, that now Preaches with us a Call to Settle as a Gofpel Minifter."

At the following meeting in April first appears any mention of Governors of the State, thus: "In order to chufe a Governor, Lieut. Governor and Senitors agreeable to the Conftitution of this Commonwealth."

In September of the same year occurs this item, "to see if the Town will take up the Vote that was Refered to a future time Concerning Mr. Huntington Porter," also "to see if the Town will Chufe a Comitee to Join with the Town of Stoughton and Stoughtonham in opening the Pafsways to let up the fish caled Alewives; to see if the Town will Raife Six men to serve at Nantafket."

In November of the same year appears, "to See if the Inhabitants will Build a New Meeting Houfe in this Town." From paying taxes for this purpose Enoch Ellis petitioned to be exempt.

Under Feb. 18, 1783, appears another attempt to settle a successor to the Rev. Phillips Payson in the Walpole church, as thus indicated:

> "To see if the Town will Unite on Giving Mr. George Morey a Call to Settle as a Gofpel Minifter in this Town and make provif on for his Settlement and Support."

The town meeting of Oct. 13, 1783, was held at the house of Samuel Fuller, innholder. At this meeting the town considered whether it would sell all pews not already disposed of, and provide means for finishing the new meeting-house. John Lewis and William Pettee were the constables and tax collectors of that year.

The town meeting of April 5, 1784, considered "a Letter from a Convention Refpecting Commutation Impofts and Cincinati." The latter being the new and popular association of the Revolutionary war officers, formed at the close of the war and still in existence.

All along, at this period, there are efforts made to separate from Suffolk County, under new auspices. This was not accomplished until Norfolk County was formed ten or more years later. The same year Seth Mann is mentioned as the town doctor, and Andrew Willett as constable.

At the May 9, 1785, town meeting was considered "to see if the Town will approve of tying Horfes to the Pofts that are Set at the corner of the Meeting Houfe."

At the Walpole meeting of Feb. 10, 1783, the following significant vote was passed: "to pay to Abner Dagget for Rum & Sugar for William Marfhall when Sick, *3s 9p.*" Rum and tobacco were then always provided for the poor, probably out of mistaken sympathy.

At the following meeting it was "voted to pay Major Bullard for serving as assessor and finding the Committee two quarts of Rum, that were appointed to open the way for the fifh to come up." Also "to Abel Allen for ufe of his houfe eleven weeks to keep School in *11s.*" "To Isaac Lewis for keeping Jonathan Dexter's wife £1 *4s.*"

At the meeting March 10, 1783, it was

> "voted to Give Mr. George Morey a call to Settle as a Gofpel Minifter with us and there was fifty-nine yeas, & nine nays."

In the winter of 1783, Major Seth Bullard and Capt. Timothy Man taught two of our schools, the latter in the south part of the town.

"May ye 12, 1783, Afsembled the Town by legal Warning and paft the following Votes, met at the Houſe Late the Property of Deacn Robbins opened the Meeting & adjourned to the Barn."

This was on account of taking down the old meeting-house the week before. At this meeting Doctor Seth Man and Doctor Jonathan Wild were chosen surveyors of highways.

May 19, 1783, it was voted "to Level the Hill for the new Meeting Houſe, by Squadrons as they took down the Meeting Houſe." Later it was voted "to procure Stone to underpin the Meeting Houſe."

May 26 it was "voted that the Meeting Houſe Stand as the old one did," and that it should have "a Steeple Raiſed when the Meeting Houſe is Raiſed," and "that Capt. Man, Benj. Hartshorn, Jona. Hidden, Lt. Gay & Lt. Willett procure Gins and Men to Raiſe the Meeting Houſe." Deep mystery surrounds this motive power.

The report of the Committee of Pew Appraisal for the new church runs thus:

"We the Subscribers being choſen by the Town a Committee to Prize the Pews and to Settle the Precedency of choice of Pews according to the Single Rate, putting two Families to a Pew have attended that Service and set them from 20 to 60 Dollars Pr Pew, the Graduation being 4 Pistireens, the first Choice falls to

		Dols.	Pistns.
1	Ephraim Clark		
	Coll. Kingsbury	60	0
2	Aaron Blake		
	James Fales	59	1
3	James Clap		
	Benja Haws	58	2
4	Nathan Kingsbury .		
	Seth Smith	57	3
5	George Payson		
	John Ellis	56	4
6	Enoch Ellis		
	Nathan Pond	56	0

No.	Name	Dols.	Pistns.
7	Widw Fales . .		
	Lt Wm. Bacon . .	55	1
8	Moses Ellis . . .		
	Aquilla Robbins . .	54	2
9	Jona Kendall . .		
	Capt Clap	53	3
10	Jofhua Allen		
	Henry Partridge . .	52	4
11	Lt Elipt. Ellis . . .		
	Enfn Boyden . . .	52	0
12	Enfn. Man . . .		
	Afa Smith	51	1
13	Esqr. Clap . . .		
	Saml Hartshorn .	50	1
14	Joshua Clap. Jr . .		
	Abner Daggett	49	3
15	Wm Robbins . .		
	Abel Allen . . .	48	4
16	Joshua Clap 3d .		
	Joshua Boyden . .	48	0
17	Joseph Gay . . .		
	Widw Gay	47	1
18	Widw Fifher .		
	Jona Hidden	46	2
19	Majr Bullard		
	Joseph Day . .	45	3
20	Mofes Smith		
	Jacob Hart	44	4
21	Jacob Clap . .		
	Ichabod Clap . . .	44	0
22	Lt Willet		
	Widw Day	43	1
23	Benja Boyden . .		
	Mofes Fales	42	2
24	Timy Hartshorn . .		
	Jeremiah Fales	41	3
25	Thos Page		
	Benja Hartshorn . . .	40	4
26	Jeremiah Day		
	Jofeph Ellis	40	0
27	Nathl Guild		
	Phillip Bardens . . .	39	1
28	Jona Boyden		
	Capt. Smith	38	2
29	Isaac Lewis		
	Saml Copp	37	3
30	Capt. Boyden		
	Benja Kingfbery . . .	36	4
31	Danl Fifher		
	Lt Benja Gay	36	0
32	Nathl Guild Jr. . . .		
	Ebenr Baker	35	1
33	Capt Man		
	Jofeph Kingsbury .	34	2
34	Richard Hartshorn .		
	Saml Boyden	33	3
35	Coll. Clap		
	Wm Bullard	32	4
36	Nicholas Harris		
	Benja. Kingsbury Jr.	32	0
37	Jofhua Morfe		
	Peter Morfe	31	1
38	John Cleaveland . . .		
	Jacob Gay	30	2
39	Seth Clap		
	Elipt Clap	29	3
40	Abner Turner		
	Lt John Boyden . . .	28	4

THE JOSEPH CARROLL—NICHOLAS HARRIS—ISAAC LEWIS, JR., PLACE, EAST WALPOLE

One of the first dwellings used for school purposes before the erection of schoolhouses

		Dols.	Pistns.
41	John Lewis		
	Saml Smith 28	28	0
42	Bezeliel Turner		
	Samuel Guild	27	1
43	Ezekiel Boyden		
	Lt Henry Partridge .	26	2
44	Ebenr Gay		
	Joseph Guild	25	3
45	Wm Pettee		
	Eleazer Clap	24	4
46	James Dupee		
	Joseph Man	24	0
47	Christopher Smith ..		
	Ebenr Hartshorn ..	23	1
48	Afa Page		
	John Boyden 3d ...	22	2
49	Lt. Benja Pettee....		
	Lt. Seth Kingsbury .	21	3
50	John Hall		
	Ebenr Day	20	4
51	Elifha Hall		
	Jofiah Hall	20	0

The last pew was afterwards owned by Richard Billings and Elijah Clap.

In September, 1783, it was voted to paint the outside of the new meeting-house, "Except the Roof." Also voted that "Mr. Morey be Defired to Come and Preach at this Town, when his time is out at Marlborough." Sept. 15, 1783, it was

"voted that thofe that have bought Pews and paid for them shall have them and their Heirs and Afsigns forever."

In 1783 Asa Kingsbury and Lois Harris taught school. Both her father's house and that of Abel Allen were used for a schoolhouse.

Although the town had passed through many complications, as in the case of paying David Farrington in 1775 for damage for closing school before his term had expired, no special mention of the word lawsuit is found in the records before June, 1785, when one is thus referred to:

"to see if the Town will grant money to carry on their Law Suit with Mofes Ellis." Enoch Ellis, Nicholas Harris, and Ezekiel Boyden were then selectmen.

Some inkling of impending trouble also appears in the following, in June, 1786:

> "3ly) for the Town to hear Reprefentation of the Selectmen Refpecting the Conduct of Mr. Nicholas Harris, who had Some of the Property of this Town Depofited in his Hands while he was one of the Selectmen the Laft year and Refufeth to deliver the Same to the Prefent Selectmen."

In the meeting of March 5, 1787, the town considered "if the Town will pay the bill of the Soldiers now Raifd or Wheather they Shall be paid by the Individuals that hired them."

At the meeting of November, 1787, the following important matter was acted upon:

> "To Chufe a Delegate to Reprefent them at a Convention to be Holden at the State Houfe in Bofton on the Second wednefday of January next to Confider of and afsent to a Late Conftitution or frame of Government."

For some reason, at this time, several articles to abate Samuel Thompson's taxes are from time to time brought into the warrant.

At the meeting "May 12, 1788, the Town voted to purchase land of Jacob and Ichabod Clap to enlarge the meeting-house common."

The old and first pound, situated on what is now West Street, was sold to Dr. Mann in 1790, and a new one constructed west of the Medfield road. This caused trouble later, when a new claimant to the old location appeared.

In 1794 also mention is made of Dr. Jonathan Wild in an abatement of taxes, and Eliphalet Rhoades, an early mill owner of East Walpole, is allowed to work out his taxes "in the croſſ Rhoad that leads by his Mill."

In June, 1794, again appears the alarm of war.

"To see if the Town will grant any pay to thoſe Men that are now detached to hold themſelves in redineſs to go into Service at the Shorteſt notice which will make up their Continental wages, three pounds per month."

In 1794 the town, under an act of the General Court, made its first survey of its territory. The map is still in the Public Archives of the State House, but is a most unsatisfactory plan of the town even as it was then.

It is a surprise to find the town then voting that eight hours shall constitute a day's labor on the roads, but there were allowed but four shillings per day.

In 1786 it was voted "that there be a fine of Six Shillings laid on each Person that shall leave or tye a Horſe within one Rod & half of the Meeting Houſe."

In 1788 Isaac Lewis was chosen constable, but hired his brother John to act in his place. Samuel Boyden was excused from working on the highway, because he "had no road to his house."

In 1788 Fisher Ames, of Dedham, as Representative to Congress, received 23 votes, Samuel Adams only 13.

In 1789 John Hancock, for Governor, received 45 votes, General Lincoln for Lieutenant Governor, 22 votes; General Heath but 3.

The following vote was passed in 1790: "to purchase a

Bell for the Meeting House at £50." A committee chosen to reckon with the town treasurer at this meeting reports: "We find in said Treafurer's hands one bad Piftereen and eighty-one bungtown Coppers." Is there as much now?

In 1792 the vote of the town for John Hancock for Governor was 68; for Samuel Adams, Lieutenant-Governor, 57.

The same year appears the following brief but comprehensive vote, "Negatived Jacks article." Jack was the slave left by Ezekiel Robbins. Just what he wanted is not known, possibly the town's sanction to a marriage with the colored woman living on West Street, who for years after went by the name of Jack's wife. Jack, at his death, was allowed a big funeral, but when living not always to carry out his own rather too primitive ideas.

In 1793 the town "voted to have a Committee of five men to pitch on and afix a place for a school Houfe in the North School District in this Town." The children of the east part of the town had been granted the choice between going to the Centre or North schools. Nathan Pond, Jr., and Isaac Lewis were chosen surveyors of highways that year.

On May 22, 1793, the town cast its first vote as a part of the county of Norfolk. It was also "voted that Capt. Oliver Clap & James Dupee be a Committee to meet at Mr. Timothy Gay's Inholder in Dedham the twelfth Day of Sept. Inft. at ten of the clock in the Morning in County Convention to tranfact Matters for the Good of the County of Norfolk."

The laying out, this year, of East Street from the old Sawmill road by the present orthodox church to Allen's corner is thus described:

"Beginning at the Bridge near Felches, at a Stake and heap of Stones in or near the wall from thence to a heap of Stones on a Small Hill thence to a Rock with Stones on the Same in land that lies undivided among the Heirs of Jonathan Fales thence Crofsing a corner of the land laid out to Stephen Fales to a Walnut tree in land set off to Mr. Briton thence to an Elm at Jofhua Allens land thence in said Allen's land till it comes to the Wefterly end of said Allen's stone Wall, so on nearly the same Courfe, till it Strikes Road near the Houfe of Ebenezer Fales Said Road to be two Rods wide."

Under April 15, 1795, the following appears: "Recd of William Bacon, Jr. and David Lewis Five Pounds, eight shillings for a Gallery Pew in the Meeting Houfe, Number five, which I have sold to them. Recd by me, Joseph Fales."

The first mention of voting for a member of Congress seems to have been on the third day of November, 1794, when it was "voted for a Perfon to Reprefent the Third Southern Diftrict in Congrefs."

In 1795 the town proposed to hire out the poor to the lowest bidder, and also to set up guide posts "at the Crotch of the Streets."

In 1796 Doctor Seth Man was engaged to ring the bell for one year at four pence a day, and the following receipt appears: "Recd of Elijah Thompson & Elezer Rhoads Twenty Five Dollars for a Pew in the Meeting Houfe Gallery. Samuel Fuller."

In 1798 the town met to "see if the Town will bear the

expenses of profecuting Eliphalet Rhoades for not serving Conftable laft year."

The arrangement about the town's poor is thus described by vote this year: The town

"to find them Cloths and Doctring in cafe of Sicknefs. Eliphalet Clap Jr took Zachariah Partridge and Wife at Nine Shillings and nine pence Pr Week. Jonathan Kendall took Jofeph Clap at two Shillings and ten pence Pr Week; Afa Hartshorn took Deborah Fales at four Shillings and four pence pr Week. Willaby Dexter took his Grandmother at three Shillings and Six pence pr Week."

"Majr Saml Hartshorn was drawn out of the box for a grand Jury man for one year."

With the exception of a brief war scare, the eighteenth century ended with Walpole undisturbed in her struggles to recover from the onerous burdens and sacrifices of the War for Independence.

At the first town meeting in 1800, Major Samuel Hartshorn was chosen moderator; Asa Kingsbury, town clerk; Major Samuel Hartshorn, Capt. Daniel Kingsbury, and Ichabod Clap, selectmen and assessors; Capt. Oliver Clap, town treasurer; Joseph Kingsbury, constable for the west and southwest, David Allen for the north and east part. It was voted to give the constables "six pence on a Pound for Collecting the Taxes."

The meeting-house was put in repair and painted, and six pews added on the lower floor and six in the gallery. These pews were sold by Major Samuel Hartshorn, acting as auctioneer. Heretofore the schoolhouses and church had been heated from a fireplace, but with the incoming nineteenth century some one was bold enough to propose a "stove and funnel," but it was promptly voted down. They had voted to discontinue food and liquors at their funerals, why should they indulge in a less warming and untried article, the stove? They wanted badly a singing school, but with like promptness it was refused. They also voted to discontinue the road that "leads by Mr. Needham's houfe." How this economy struck Mr. Needham we can only imagine.

In 1801, however, the town, coming to its senses,

> "voted to have a Road by Mr. Needham's houfe in which Elijah Clap now lives over the bridge that is now torn partly away, and to have the Selectmen lay the same out and prize the land which was taken from the Widow payfon for a part of the fd Road."

The Mr. Needham in question was John Needham, who afterwards ran the stage route from Boston to Providence through North Walpole and the Plain, in close rivalry with the stage line which passed through East Walpole, stopping at the half-way house in South Walpole.

Both were Boston and Providence lines, and both had half-way houses in Walpole. Needham's was just this side of the Horace Guild place on the Plain. He purchased, at one time, the old Brass Ball Tavern, to prevent any rivalry on his line in sale of refreshments.

The Payson land was what for years was known as the schoolhouse pasture, and included the Deacon Willard Lewis place.

It will be remembered that the Rev. Phillips Payson gave this land to the town as long as it should be used for school purposes, and that Deacon Ezekiel Robbins erected a small one-story school building thereon, which was afterwards moved to the south end of the premises. Here the writer's father, in his boyhood, was obliged to come to school all the way from the east part of the town.

At this town meeting it was also "Granted for to hire a room and for Candles & fire wood for the ufe of Singers in this Town the prefent year £10."

The matter of stage routes above referred to was first brought to the attention of Walpole at the town meeting of Jan. 11, 1802. It was then

> "voted to act on the petition of Esqr Starkweather and others refpecting a turn pike. Voted to object againft a turnpike coming through this town. Voted to have the Selectmen draw up a remonftrance to send by Mr. Bacon to the General Court, and to have him ufe his influence againft a turnpike going through this town."

When we reflect that there was no public conveyance in those days, we marvel somewhat at this unwise obstruction of such a useful progress.

There had been a post over the old post-road a little to the east of Walpole territory, passing over the Neponset River at King's bridge (Morrill's in Norwood), stopping at White's just south, at Roebuck Tavern, the Gould neighborhood, at Billings' in West Sharon, and on to Providence. General Lafayette and other well-known public characters used this route, stopping in East Walpole. There is an interesting account by Madam Sarah Knight, who traveled over this route in 1704.

It may be of interest to many to read the following layout of the Needham road above referred to:

"Walpole, Feb. 19th, 1802. We the Subſcribers met and laid out a Road by Elijah Clap to the great Road and make the following Report (viz.) begining a little diſtance from the Centre School houſe runing as the wall now stands to the River the ſaid road to be southerly of said wall thence Croſſing the River to the wall the ſoutherly ſide of ſaid road, thence on ſaid wall till it comes near a pear tree, then turning a ſtrait Courſe on to the top of the hill near an Apple-tree to the Great road, the ſaid road laid out three Rods wide, alſo that Mr. John Needham gives the land, the weſt ſide of the river for the road and gives a piece of land to the heirs of Dea. George payſon, deceaſed, which the ſaid heirs have improved in the room of the land taken for the ſaid Road the Eaſterly ſide of the River and the Common between the Roads for the towns uſe."

On March 1, 1802, it was "voted to accept Ebenr Baker with his real Eſtate to be Annexed to this Town." This year the town gave 48 votes for "his Excelency Caleb Strong, Governor."

On April 4, 1803, it was "voted to have the Selectmen agree with some Perſon to Ring the Bell and at funerals of defeased by the Relations at the towns expense." This custom has only recently been discontinued.

On April 2, 1804, it was voted to accept "Danl Fiſhers Road" (Fisher Street) and to give "50 dol towards making the fence." Also "to give Jotham Morſe 10 dollars towards ſupporting his mother Gregory."

At the meeting April 15, 1804, first appears a political name affixed to the Governor.

The electors at large for choice of President are: "Republicans, Hon. James Sullivan (Governor), Hon. Elbridge Gerry; Federals, Hon. David Cobb, Hon. Oliver Wendell."

In May, 1805, came the struggle over the construction of the Joshua Allen road. Why there should have been such strong opposition is not known.

On May 2, 1808, it was voted to furnish the Walpole Light Infantry with powder and ball. And, alas! on Nov. 7, 1808, it was

"Voted to have the Selectmen Carry Hannah Jack to Jail at Dedham, if she behave well in their opinion they may neglect to Carry her to Dedham Jail."

Thus again we see that Ezekiel Robbins's slave legacy shows its unsavory side.

On March 6, 1809, it was "voted to make an addition to the pay of those men detached for the Service of the U. States provided they are called for, they are to be made up by said town to the Sum of Twelve Dollars with the States' pay, and two Dollars bounty."

The vote for Levi Lincoln for Governor this year was 116, for Christopher Gore 80.

On March 4, 1811, it was "voted to build a powder houfe seven feet one way, and eight the other and to built with Brick, by David Lewis, Daniel Allen and Nathan Ware."

In 1814 John A. Gould, who ever afterwards was a prominent citizen, and at one time, when Walpole tried to be the shire town, a candidate for judge of probate, was excused from serving as constable.

On May 1, 1815, the town accepted the "road from Ruben Allens to Capt. David Allen's & thence to the Norfolk & Bristol turnpike." This was Peach street.

In 1825 there seems to have been no clearly established bounds to the "meeting house common," or the Common as it is now called. Committee after committee were chosen to fix some definite limit, but before it was settled another far more important question arose, which is foreshadowed in the following vote:

"March 6, 1826. Voted to choose a committee of five to confer with the Reverend George Morey to afcertain if he will difsolve his ministerial connection with the town, and on what terms. Chose Harvey Boyden, Joshua Stetson, Harvey Clap, Asa Whitman, & Joseph Carroll for the Committee."

At the April meeting their report was read and it was voted to obtain legal advice and see how far the town's agreement with Mr. Morey was binding.

Also at this meeting a school committee of five persons was chosen. They were our first school committee, and were Ebenezer Stone, John A. Gould, Harvey Ruggles, David Morse, and Daniel Kingsbury.

On May 1, 1826, it was

"Voted that it is the wish of the Town to difsolve the ministerial connection with the Rev. George Morey. Moved that a Committee of seven be chosen to wait on the Rev. George Morey and to offer him an opportunity to make any propositions which he may wish, to the town of Walpole through them in relation to a disolution of his Ministerial contract with them, and should he make any, which, in their opinion might be deemed proper, to request the Selectmen to call a meeting of the town, and then & there to lay said proposition before the town. Should he not make to them any propositions said Committee then propose to Mr. Morey a mutual council, and, in case he should reject a mutual council, that said committee forth with proceed to convoke an ex parte council. Voted in the affirmative. Chofe for said Committee Capt Joshua Stetson, Harvey Boyden, Timothy Mann, Joseph Hawes, Joseph Ellis, Warren Clap, Asa Whitman."

On May 15, 1826, this committee reported and it was then

"Voted, Whereas the Rev. George Morey has now for upwards of forty two years regularly officiated in the office of minister over the church and society in the town, and whereas by reason of the decay of his strength and the infirmities of age, he has become unable to discharge the duties of said office, and whereas it is extremely desirable for the continued peace and quietude of the town, and will be conducive to the comfort and welfare of our venerable Pastor as well as to that of the people, that a final arrangement & adjustment should take place with him in relation to his Salary before measures are taken towards employing some suitable candidate to preach the Gospel amongst us, & whereas our said Pastor has signified a willingnefs to enter into an arrangement which shall consist with what he owes himself & with the honor & reputation of the town. Therefore voted that the town pay the Rev. George Morey the sum of six hundred Dollars in full for all future claims for his stipulated Salary, and that the same committee, who were appointed at the last meeting on the subject, be hereby authorized to carry said vote into effect, and to adjust the manner in which he shall release said claim & in which he shall be relieved from the discharge of the duties of his office & to do all such things in the case as the interest and welfare of the town and proper respect and regard to the feelings of the Rev Mr. Morey require. Voted to grant six hundred Dollars to pay Rev. George Morey and Ministerial uses. Voted to choose a committee of nine to supply the desk."

AGREEMENT

This agreement between George Morey of Walpole in the County of Norfolk, Clerk, & the Church & Christian Society in said Town, Witnefseth, That the said Morey doth hereby agree to preach no longer and hereby retires from the discharge of the active duties of minister over said Church & society & hence forth will cease to officiate in any way as minister in the desk or meeting house in said Town, & doth relinquish & give up all claim to any salary or stipulated annual sum & doth release the Town or people from all obligation to pay him the same or any sum henceforth, & the said Town doth agree to relieve said Morey from the discharge of the duties of minister & that he shall not be required to do any act or perform labour on account of his retaining the character of minister, & the Town have this day paid him six hundred dollars in full for his relinquishment of his salary as aforesaid, & it is understood that the said Morey is to continue to enjoy the privileges, perquisites & immunities of a settled minister of the Gospel in said Town, & is to be entitled to the respect and standing of such minister except so far as the relinquishment within extends; And it is understood that the said Morey shall receive his former stipulated salary up to the fifteenth day of May 1826, & it is understood to be the intention of said Town to employ some one to preach in said Morey's place, and in due time, if practicable, to settle a suitable person as colleague with said Morey, it is understood that said Morey & the church & society in Walpole shall henceforth cultivate those sentiments of mutual respect & esteem & shall so demean themselves that the peace & harmony of the Town will be promoted, that no interference with each shall occur, but the best disposition & mutual friendship shall be cherished. In witness whereof the parties aforesaid have hereunto set their hands this fifteenth day of May in the year of our Lord 1826.

TIMOTHY MANN, JOSHUA STETSON, HARVEY BOYDEN, ASA WHITMAN, JOSEPH HAWES, JOSEPH ELLIS, WARREN CLAP.
Committee of the Town Authorized by a vote of the same.

Attest
DANIEL KINGSBURY
DAVID COBB

Attest
PALMER MOREY
PRISALLER MOREY.

GEORGE MOREY, *Clerk.*"

How much this occurrence had to do with the approaching division of the church and parish, which led to the formation of the Orthodox church and society, cannot now be judged. It must have created an opportunity if not an excuse as public feeling was deeply stirred.

On July 31, 1826, it was by the town

"Voted that we highly approve of the recommendation of the church of the Rev. J. P. B. Storer, as a person well and suitably qualified to be elected to the office of a public teacher of Piety, Religion and Morality, over the Church and religious society in this town. Voted that a committee be chosen and instructed to invite the Rev Mr Storer to settle over us in said character and to offer him an annual salary of the sum of six hundred Dollars upon the condition however that either party shall have the liberty to recede from their contract by giving in writing six months notice of their intention so to do. If a dissolution of the contract be wished for on the part of the town, and the citizens thereof being duly and legally afsembled for that purpose, and it being so declared by a majority of the voters present, then there shall be a second town meeting called for the same purpose within fourteen days thereafter, and if after a majority of the voters present shall adhere to their former vote for a difsolution of the contract, and a copy of said vote being given to the Rev. Mr. Storer, it shall operate as a difsolution of the contract at the expiration of six months thereafter. If a difsolution of said contract be desired by the Rev. Mr Storer, a notice of his request in writing lodged with the town clerk, shall operate as a difsolution of the contract at the expiration of the time aforesaid, and the said committee shall report at some future meeting their doings together with the answer of the Rev. Mr Storer to the propositions contained in this note. Daniel Kingsbury, Timothy Mann, Joshua Stetson, Daniel Allen, and Harvey Boyden were appointed said committee.

Attest HARVEY CLAP, *Town Clerk.*"

On Oct. 2, 1826, it was "voted to choose a committee of

nine whose duty it shall be to make all suitable arrangements for the ordination. Chose for said committee, Daniel Kingsbury, Joshua Stetson, Harvey Boyden, Henry Plimpton, Nathan Carroll, Joseph Hawes, Oliver Lincoln, Truman Clarke, Isaac Bullard."

"The doeing of the Ecclistastical Council convened at Walpole Nov 15, 1826. At a council convened by Letters missive from the church of Christ in Walpole at Walpole on the 15 Nov. 1826, present the following churches: 1, Portland, Dr. Nichols & Judge W. P. Preble; 2, West Boston Dr. Lowell & E. P. Hartshorn; 3, Federal St. pastor E. S. Gannett & F. A. Failes; 4, Hollis St. Mr. Pierpoint & Deacon S. May; 5, Seed Church H. Ware & J. A. Eams; 6, Brookline Dr Pierce and Joshua C. Clark; 7, Dorchester 1st church Dr Harris & Dea. Eb. Clapp; 8 Dorchester 3d Church Dr. Richmond & Hon John Baily; 9, Medfield Dr Sanders & P. Allen; 10, Sherborn, Mr Townsend and Dea Dan Leland; 11, Medway, Mr Bailey & Dea Jon Blake; 12, Dover Mr. Sanger & Josiah Newell; 13, Needham Mr Ritchie and Dea. Jonathan Newell & Rev. Mr Kimball; 14, Dedham, Mr. Lamson & Dea Eliphalet Baker; 15, Dedham 2nd Church Mr White & Dea John Richards; 16, Mansfield, Elkanah Bates; 17, Norton Mr Clark & Eph Raymond; 18, Providence Dr Edes & Dea John C. Jenks; 19, Mr Dewey & Dea M. Kempton; 20th, Canton, Mr. Huntoon & Genl Crane; 21, North Bridgwater Dea John Perkins & Col Caleb Howard; 22, Roxbury 1st Church Dr. E. Porter."

The proceedings of the church and society, relative to the invitation to the pastor-elect, together with his reply thereto, were laid before the council and read by the scribe. The proceedings between the Rev. Mr. Morey, late pastor of the town and church, were produced and read by the scribe, whereupon the following motion was made by Hon. Judge Preble:

"WALPOLE, NOV. 15, 1826.

"In Ecclesiastical Council convened the day and year aforesaid. Whereas the Rev. George Morey of Walpole, in consequence of his advanced age and increasing infirmities, has by mutual agreement between himself & the church and Christian society over which he was Settled and ordained, retired from the discharge of the active duties of minister over said church and Society, & ceased henceforth to officiate in any way as minister in the desk or meeting in said Town, & will preach no longer; but the said Morey, is to continue to enjoy the privileges, perquisites and immunities of a settled minister of the Gospel, in no way however interfering with the active pastoral duties — and whereas said church and Christian Society have elected the Rev. J. P. B. Storer to the pastoral office over said Church & Society to take upon himself, without interference from the said Morey, the whole pastoral duties with the Sole reservation herein exprefsed. Voted this council does fully approve & concur in the arrangements between the Rev. Mr. Morey and his church & Christian Society."

The pastor-elect presented certificates of regular standing as a member of a Christian church, and of approbation as a candidate for the ministry.

"Voted that this council is satisfied of the regularity of proceedings of this church & Society in their call to Mr. Storer, and with the documents and testimonials presented by the Pastor elect."

Hon. Judge Preble read the following communication from the pastor-elect:

"WALPOLE, NOV. 15, 1826.

"*To the Reverend, the Ecclesiastical Council Afsembled in this place.*

"The undersigned asks leave respectfully to state to your reverend body, that such are his views of duty, and of the principles by which ministers of our Lord should be governed, he never could suffer himself to remain the Pastor of a people alienated from him in affection and opposed to him in his ministeriel office. He has therefore taken this mode of thus publickly declaring, that whenever a majority of the whole number of legal voters who statedly worship with the religious society in this town over which he is about to be settled and ordained, & who actually contribute for the Support of the Gospel by paying taxes towards his Salary shall desire his ministerial connection with them to be difsolved, & such desire shall be ascertained & expresfed in legal meeting by the requisite number, a majority of the whole number of all the legal voters in the society, voting for such difsolution, he will waive everything in the condition of settlement made between himself and the Town requiring two thirds of the voters present at a legal meeting to difsolve his ministerial connection with his people.

"J. P. B. Storer."

The communication having been read,

"Voted. Resolved, as the sense of this council, that we fully and cordially approve and sanction the principles stated by Mr. Storer in his note of this day, addrefsed to this body, in relation to the terms and conditions of his settlement in the Ministry with his people.

"Voted that the Council is ready to proceed to the public Services of the ordination. Voted that the Council approve of and unite in the appointment of the Rev Mr. Huntoon to give the right hand of fellowship.

"Voted that Dr. Harris be requested to make the ordaining prayer & Mr White the concluding prayer.

"Signed Eliphalet Porter, Moderator."

Thus was an extremely delicate and dangerous public condition in a measure acceptably removed.

In 1827 Daniel Webster received but ten votes for Governor, and Samuel Hoar but four. It is impossible now, after long years of political worship, to account for this apparent lack of appreciation.

It was voted this year "that the land whereon the town pound is now located shall be the property of Harlow

Lawrence, provided the said Lawrence shall furnish another good and sufficient pound." This was the first pound, and long in dispute. This was settled by giving the location south of the Medfield road, where it remained until a few years ago and was our last pound, the old one being on West Street. Dr. Mann at one time claimed the old site, hence this vote of the town.

In 1827 the town voted to defend against a suit of John Blackburn. This suit grew out of the dissolution of the contract between the town and the Rev. Mr. Morey. As has been seen, $600 was voted to purchase freedom from life-long support of the old pastor. This money had to be raised by taxation. One of our citizens, John Blackburn, was present at the town meeting that voted the money, and stated that it was not enough, that it should have been $1000. By the time the tax collector got around, however, Mr. Blackburn had taken an opposite view and refused at first to pay anything, but finally settled and brought suit to recover it back, but lost his case.

There have been not a few town suits which, like the one in question, have stirred the community to its very foundation, notably, Walpole *vs.* Gray, which was a closely contested political quarrel over school money. It was finally settled by the defendant, but has never yet been settled in the minds of the public.

This case was years after followed by Stone *vs.* Walpole, and recently by Walpole *vs.* the Massachusetts Chemical Company. All of these cases have settled important matters and established legal precedents for all like cases.

The latter case was decided according to what has always been regarded the true state of facts, that neither Blackburn nor any one claiming under him had anything but a mere winter's flowage. As that was granted on the ground of mutual and general benefit, the subsequent failure on the part of the owner of the privilege for nearly a century to do his part, ought, in good conscience and justice, to release from all lands flowed any easement or further obligation whatsoever. People who, out of natural goodness of heart, accommodate their less fortunate neighbors should never be imposed upon.

The Common had long been a subject of discussion. Twice it had been graded after the removal of the little knoll of early days. In 1829, the town gratefully accepted its second enlargement, under the following vote: "Voted to accept of the land offered by Capt. Warren Clap and others for a common, and smooth and level the same in such a manner that it shall be safe and convenient passing over the same, the expense of doing the same not to exceed two hundred dollars."

At the meeting May 3, 1830, it was "voted that the custom of offering and receiving ardent spirits as a token of hospitality is injurious in its tendency and ought to be abolished."

The school committee chosen for the year 1831 were Rev. John P. B. Storer, Rev. Asahel Bigelow, Ebenezer Stone, Truman Clarke, and Joshua Stetson, Jr. The schools, by that time, were firmly established. The old schoolhouse at what is now the west end of the Common was supplanted by a two-story building on Ebenezer

Clap's land, where the Methodist Church now stands, and soon after the dwelling-house of Deacon Willard Lewis erected by Capt. Horatio Wood. It has been claimed by our fathers that a part of the small tenement house to the southwest of the Lewis place, sometimes called the Gay house, is the identical old school building.

Nearly all the other schoolhouses have undergone a like change. The North has been moved from the Deacon Fisher neighborhood down to Main Street. The East schoolhouse, a long one-story building, from the rear end of which rose a small brick chimney, had its only door (a green one) a little to the left of the centre of its front, offset by a front window with red wooden shutters. It had also four windows on each side, each protected by the same red wooden shutters. As you entered, there was a vestibule, one end of which was utilized as a wood-house. Passing to the right, there was the school-room door. Around the side and rear walls of the room was a continuous board seat, and separated therefrom by an aisle were the centre forms and board seats, all in dull lead color. At the front left-hand corner, on a small raised platform, stood a small high desk and seat of the teacher. It first stood on the Fifth Sawmill dividend, on land of Mr. Allen, just above and opposite the premises of the writer.

On the increased growth of this part of the town it was moved to the north end of the present school grounds, where, for years, it sat facing the north. It was not long, however, before John and George Burt, of Mattapan, were hired to erect its successor and the predecessor of the present school buildings.

JOSHUA STETSON, JR.

Prominent manufacturer; Town Clerk from 1831 to 1845; member of the School Board for years, and in 1836, 1837, and 1838 our Representative in General Court

WALPOLE'S FIRST TWO-STORIED SCHOOLHOUSE

This stood on the site of the present Methodist Church, Walpole Centre. The successor of the old first school building, and the scene of the writer's second school-teaching experience and that of many able instructors of the time

A notable "School Dame" of the old Walpole schools
MISS MARY ROBICHAUX

A pupil of Miss Robichaux and teacher of Principal Albert Boyden of the Bridgewater Normal School

PRISCILLA G. LEWIS

Wife of Calvin G. Plimpton

Much might be added concerning the schools and their different buildings, but it would require a volume in itself. Besides the teachers already mentioned were Miss Robichaux, some of whose pupils are still living; Abigail Guild, still living, the last of a worthy family; John, Fannie, Martha, Priscilla, Harriet, Clara, Elizabeth, and Isaac Newton Lewis; Albert Boyden, Miss Boyden, Mr. Hyde, G. M. Hollingsworth, Henry Holmes, Mary H. Holder; Burgess Park, Mark Manahan, Schiller Horsford, Martha and Fanny Perkins; Andrew Washburn, Ella Bacon, Martha Metcalf, Sarah J. Morey, Miss Mann, Ellen and Ann Metcalf, Bainbridge Morey, Carrie A. Plimpton, Leonard Walker, Lizzie Robbins, Emily Chickering, Harriet M. Johnson, Clara F. Allen, Emily Mann, Olive Gray, Mary Morey, and many others, who deserve to be gratefully remembered. The same can be said of the town's school committee, although the State Board of Education of the present year reports that the school boards of the State were never so inferior and inefficient. The advice of our chairman in 1862 should be heeded. He says:

> "We beg you, fellow citizens, give to the Committee this cooperation and the confidence which must inspire it. If we are not entitled to this confidence and cooperation, put in our places those who are. But as you love your children and would prepare them to meet the responsibilities of the future, watch over, support and cherish our system of Free Public Schools."

In 1802 the Walpole Light Infantry was formed under Capt. Samuel Fales, with high leather chapeau with silvered brass mountings and sheeptail cockade, and the small haversack, with its W. L. I. This heavy hat gave way afterwards to a cap, and the heavy flintlock to one more light and trim.

Down to the Revolutionary War the old matchlock was in common use. It was so heavy as to require a rest in firing. It is no wonder that it often proved more disastrous to the owner than the foe. His whole family might easily be tomahawked and scalped before the unwieldy and uncertain firearm could be made effective.

Capt. Warren Clap commanded this Light Infantry in the 1812 War, on its march to Boston and the coast.

In the fall of 1814 our grandfathers were called out to again repel the British.

ROSTER OF CAPTAIN WARREN CLAP'S CO., COL. VALENTINE'S REGIMENT, MASS. MILITIA IN WAR OF 1812–14, CALLED OUT BY THE GOVERNOR TO REPEL A THREATENEL INVASION. SERVICE RENDERED AT BOSTON FROM SEPTEMBER 10 TO OCTOBER 30, 1814. COMPANY RAISED IN WALPOLE AND VICINITY

Warren Clap, Captain
Samuel Mason, Lieutenant
Daniel Hartshorn, Ensign
Harvey Boyden, Sergt
Henry Plimpton, Sergt
Otis Hartshorn, Sergt
Pitts Smith, Sergt
Daniel Boyden, Musician
Horace Guild, Musician
Lewis Guild, Musician
Joseph W. Gray, Musician
Jason Williams, Musician
Daniel Allen, Private
Reuben Allen, Private
Samuel Allen, Private
Warren Allen, Private
Jason Boyden, Private
Warren Boyden, Private
Bradish Clap, Private
Curtis Clap, Private
Josiah Day, Private
Jeremiah Day, Jr., Private
Willard Ellis, Private
Lewis Fales, Private
Abijah Fales, Private
Josiah Hill, Private
Josiah Hall, Private
Willard Hall, Private

AN OFFICER IN THE OLD WALPOLE LIGHT INFANTRY

One of Parson Morey's young men. An organizer of the original Orthodox Society, its first organist, and the father of John W. Lewis. Sergt. William Lewis, third cousin of Sergt. William Lewis of Capt. William Bacon's Crown Point Company in 1755–56

JOHN W. LEWIS

Eminent conductor, composer, and teacher of both vocal and instrumental music

Richard Hartshorn, Private	Ziba Plimpton, Private
Isaac Lewis, Private	Daniel Plimpton, Private
Aaron Lewis, Private	Elias Plimpton, Private
John Lewis, Private	John A Pond, Private
Jason Lewis, Private	Joseph Robbins, Private
Samuel Mann, Private	Jeremiah Smith, Private
Wm Mann, Private	Daniel Turner, Private

This company had prior service at Dorchester Heights. Captain Baldwin, after whom our well-known apple was called, was called to defend East Boston at the same time. The writer still retains his grandfather's old wooden canteen, gun, and uniform of this 1812 War.

The war with Mexico, in 1845, had very little to do with us here, except an increased interest in politics and in the militia in which the Walpole Light Infantry shone in all its glory. One of its old canvas tents was, down to the Civil War, used yearly for fall seaside outings at Squantum, to the great joy of us children.

At this period, the old-fashioned singing-school was in full favor, and with candy-pulls and moonlight skating furnished almost the only recreation of the time. In hall and vestry on the long winter nights, both young and old drank of the ever refreshing fountain with a heartiness and satisfaction impossible of belief to the present generation. Horace Bird, Handel Pond, John W. Lewis, E. M. Metcalf, William R. Smith, and others, were ever ready to entertain the old and instruct the young in that almost holy calling.

CHAPTER IX

MANY were the misgivings, however, on the agitation of the extension of slave territory. The settlement of Kansas by lovers of human freedom received from but a very few here its due attention.

William Lloyd Garrison, Theodore Parker, and a very few others, for years, were the only active consciences America showed, and even to the unhappy ending of the deplorable raid of the sturdy abolitionist, John Brown, at Harper's Ferry. Although, among the more humble classes, sympathy and manliness raised many a true friend to the negro, few openly expressed their convictions.

The writer recalls, even now, the almost doomlike silence and dread when Francis W. Bird, an early disciple of Garrison, boldly draped the columns and front of his mill office, in the east part of the town, in respect and grief for that untimely fall of slavery's great martyr, John Brown of Osawatomie.

Nor was the feeling materially different before the murderous onslaught on Charles Sumner in the capitol at Washington. Preston Brooks little imagined the coming effect of those cruel blows.

Sumner, in the eyes of fast increasing numbers here, stood forth not only the foremost champion of the down-

HON. F. W. BIRD ON LEAVING BROWN UNIVERSITY

trodden slave, but their most glorious martyr. And when, after his recovery to temporary health, he came to Walpole, the whole country around eagerly flocked to hear and see him.

The old orthodox church was unable to hold the throng. Settees were placed closely in the vestibule and aisles. There was not even standing room, and from the beginning to the end of that speech every eye feasted on its hero in almost deathlike silence.

From that time on the enslaved negro did not lack here sympathetic friends. The temperance question, which under the name of the Washingtonian Movement, in which Rev. Edwin Thompson was prominent, had for years absorbed all others, in a trice gave way to that of universal freedom. It is impossible for the present generation to realize the intensity or sacredness of our experience then.

There was bitter feeling, however, after the Fremont unsuccessful campaign. Men who had large interests in the iron and cabinet trade with the South and West began to be severe in their excited denunciation of the slave and of abolitionism. It was a common retort by even members of the churches that the blood of the imminent struggle would, at the judgment, be upon the skirts of the Abolitionist and all his sympathizers. And, ever increasing, the excitement continued till the election of Abraham Lincoln, when all, even the Republicans, began to see to what the country was tending. The huge wooden axes of Lincoln and Hamlin societies suddenly turned into iron and steel.

The shot on Sumter alone returned our town to a sane

and worthy patriotism. The President's call for three-months men met with ready response. Men, boys, caught the war fever. Nor did our disaster at Bull Run much change the deep sentiment. It rather deepened their ardor and strengthened their courage.

Daily young men left the shop, counting-room, and fields for Boston, and gaily returned with a ribbon in their buttonhole, quietly explaining that they had enlisted. Fortunate those who again returned to peaceful life.

The remains of E. Brigham Piper, Martin Fisher, Lieut. Henry Godbold, and others early brought home here saddened but did not weaken our lively patriotism. Fairs, apple-paring bees, and lint depositaries busily furnished supplies for the hospital and the field. Hardly a family of any size but was represented in the ranks.

The tablets placed in our town hall to commemorate our sacrifices in the long war for freedom and the integrity of the nation read as follows:

The citizens of Walpole, honoring the faithful services of their sons in aiding to suppress Rebellion, and maintain the integrity of the Nation, have erected these tablets:

In Memoriam

Elbridge B. Piper, died April 18, 1862, in hospital at Newburne, N. C.

John W. Frizell, died May 18, 1862, in hospital at Port Royal, S. C.

Patrick Herne, killed in battle at Bull Run, Aug. 30, 1862.

John E. McKew, killed in battle at Fredericksburg, Va., Dec. 13, 1862.

Henry L. Godbold died in hospital at Washington, D. C., Sept. 27, 1862, of wounds received in battle.

Martin L. Fisher, died Aug. 18, 1862, in New York.

James S. Gilmore, died Feb. 26, 1863, in hospital.

William C. Manter, died Feb. 13, 1863, in hospital at Fairfax, Va.

John G. Woods, died June 30, 1864, in hospital at City Point.

Samuel Jackson, died July 6, 1864, in hospital at Washington, D. C., of wounds received in battle.

Charles N. Spear, died Oct. 29, 1864, in hospital at Newburne, N. C.

Lowell E. Hartshorn, died Dec. 16, 1864, in Andersonville Prison, Ga.

Roll of Honor — 1861–1865

David W. Lewis, Capt. Vt. 9th Regt.
Henry L. Godbold, 1st Lieut. 1st Penn. Artillery
Silas E. Stone, Asst. Surgeon, 23d Mass. Regt.
Samuel N. Piper, q.m. Sergt. 23d Mass. Regt.
James W. Bacon, Sergt. 33d Mass. Regt.
Jason Lewis, Sergt. 46th Mass. Regt.
Charles N. Spear, Corp. 23d Mass. Regt.
John W. Frizell, Corp. 28th Mass. Regt.
Wm. F. Drugan, Regt. 1.
John M. Drugan, Regt. 2.
Henry W. Stevens, Regt. 7.
Patrick E. Driscoll, Regt. 12.
Charles E. Leland, Regt. 13.

Regiment 18

George H. F. Alford
George W. Lewis
John Wiggin
John H. Smith
Patrick Herne
N. H. F. Richardson
John McGinnis
George E. Dorethy
Job. Ramsbottom

Regiment 23

Edward Clinton
Warren Bacon
M. B. Hartshorn
Warren Mylod
Elbridge B. Piper
Melzar W. Allen
Daniel G. Shepard
S. S. Hartshorn
Joshua Allen
Harlin P. Baker
Patrick Flood
Battalion 16

REGIMENT 26

Henry F. Achorn

William T. Reeney

REGIMENT 33

James E. Blackington
James A. Daggett
John Daily
Michael Griffin
Lewis A. Hall

John C. Nickerson
Silas W. Nickerson
Fred Sheridan
George W. Young

REGIMENT 35

John E. McKew

REGIMENT 39

Benjamin M. Briggs

REGIMENT 42

Ebenezer B. Park
Simon E. Fisher
George W. Gay
George H. Gill

Milton E. Fales
Patrick E. Kirby
Thomas Shea (26)
Paul V. Smith

Ira Fisher

REGIMENT 44

Albion G. Achorn
Asa W. Bowditch
Nathan W. Fisher
James S. Gilmore
James E. Hutchinson
Charles J. Rhodes
Josiah Fowler
Stephen T. Baker
Henry C. Fuller

Willard M. Babbitt
Robert H. Duff
Albert Fisher
Lowell E. Hartshorn
George W. Nickerson
Henry A. Thomas
Winslow E. Brown
Horace B. Hartshorn
Francis H. Fales

Charles L. Gray
Luman W. Gilmore
Fred A. Hartshorn
John A. Nudd
Edwin B. Ridge
Francis A. Tisdale
James A. Lewis
Horace A. Spear
Patrick Kindehan

REGIMENT 56

Edward R. Allen
George H. Morse

REGIMENT 58

Samuel Jackson

REGIMENT 59

John C. Woods

CAVALRY 1

Martin L. Fisher

BATTERY 1

James E. Hopkins

CAVALRY 4

Patrick Ryan
Michael Kinney
Winfield H. Scott

CAVALRY 5

John Brown

BATTERY 11

Frank L. Boyden

BATTERY 14

Wallace Kenny

Battery 16

John E. Earley
James A. Boyden
Robert W. Stevens
Julius Boyden
James A. Battersby
James A. Mitchell

1st. R. I. Artillery

William G. Manter
Albert F. Merrill
John Campbell
William H. Lyon
John A. Gray
John Higgins
Horace C. Briggs

U. S. Navy

Samuel E. Guild
Philo Bailey
Jason E. Cowden
Charles H. Hickox
Oniaslion Kaufman
Joseph Luce
Michael Robison
George A. Russell
Martin Thomas
William Spain
John McCarty
Thomas Ryon
George D. Campbell
Frederick A. Griffen
Henrich Beeker
Charles H. Haskell
Frank Hotchkiss
George Mansfield
Morten Personlius
Norman A. Sacket
Alex T. Rummalls
Frederick Lumberd
Moses Day
Isaac Hixon
Mark Glann
Albin M. Piper

DEACON HENRY PLIMPTON

Father of Calvin G. and Henry M. Plimpton

CHAPTER X

THE town of Walpole was, as can be seen from the foregoing, separated from the mother town, Dedham, solely on the matter of convenience, the convenience of managing affairs of both town and church. Home was its foundation, the church and school its immediate superstructure.

Its first minister, the Rev. Joseph Belcher, owing to domestic difficulties, after a few years of earnest and laborious work, without a church building and without proper support, holding his little flock together in any dwelling offered for the purpose, soon left town for a Southern field of labor.

His successor, the Rev. Phillips Payson, came to town on June 8, 1729 (old style), and remained, through a lifelong ministry of some 48 years, our only minister, dying Jan. 22, 1778.

He was thrice married, his wives being, first, Anne Swift, of Framingham; second, the widow Kezia Morse, of Medfield; and the third, the widow Sarah Mather, of Pomfret, a kinswoman.

His family were of more than common ability, and the town should entertain for them more than the usual regard vouchsafed to those of the early past. The sons

Phillips, John, Samuel, and Seth especially lay claim to our respect and admiration. The family has been so fully referred to in a recent address by the writer, it is needless to more than casually refer to it here.

For some years after the Rev. Phillips Payson's death, the town chose no successor. He had lived through two wars that severely taxed the country's resources, and had seen approaching the coming though deplored struggle for independence. His remains rest in the old Walpole cemetery on Main Street, a little north of his old parsonage.

After enjoying the ministration of the Rev. Huntington Porter for some time, an attempt to settle him was made, but defeated.

It was not until the Rev. George Morey appeared, March 10, 1783, that the town seemed willing to again settle any one.

With him came also a new meeting-house, sixty feet long, and forty feet wide. All the material of the old building suitable was used in the new. In 1791 a bell was placed in the belfry. There was an eastern and a western entrance.

Mr. Morey, also, was a graduate of Harvard College, a man of culture and of striking peculiarities. It is said that he used a system of cipher in writing his sermons so that none but he could read and use them. It is also reported that he, just before his death, destroyed pretty much all his manuscripts, but when his old home on the Medfield road was destroyed by fire a few years ago, it was said that a collection of his old sermons and some books, bricked up in the old chimney, were included in the ruins.

He wore the regular cocked hat, long queue fastened by a ribbon, knee breeches and pumps, to the last, and carried in his advanced age a substantial cane, the bane of many a youth he stopped on the street to catechize.

He had the street from the meeting-house to his home straightened, improved, and bounded on each side by a suitable fence, at the town's expense, and over the short way he used to drive in horse and chaise, starting for church at the first sound of the bell. His old horse, as familiar with the call from the church tower as his master's "kedup," when one day, it is said, the reverend gentleman failed to approach his carriage with his usual punctuality, immediately set out for the church alone, and on arriving at the meeting-house, after waiting sufficiently for his master's alightment, appropriately moved on to his shed behind.

It is left to imagination to depict what was the impression made on the mind and feelings of Mr. Morey on this occasion.

On one occasion one of his church was discussing with deep concern the subject of universal sin, and was much taken by surprise by his pastor's volunteered advice that he had better go home and consider his own sins, and he would have plenty to occupy his officious attention for one while. There is no doubt the good man's weakness was keenly touched.

There was formed during this period the first Library Association, which soon developed into a Historical Society. Before the Rev. Mr. Morey died, July 26, 1829, a colleague was chosen, Nov. 15, 1826, in the Rev. John

P. B. Storer, also a graduate of Harvard College, and of a more than usual inquiring and progressive mind. This led him, like William Ellery Channing, Theodore Parker, and others, to absorb much new thought which soon led to Unitarianism.

This led ultimately to the first division of the old church and society. Those still clinging to the old ideas of the Trinity petitioned for a separation so that they might worship according to the dictates of their own consciences, but before the petition was granted they withdrew, and on Oct. 4, 1826, met together and subscribed to the following agreement:

"We, the subscribers, heretofore members of the Congregational Society in Walpole, lately under the pastoral care of the Rev. George Morey, do hereby manifest our secession from said society, and do agree, by setting our signature hereunto, to unite in forming another religious society in said Town of Walpole by the name of the Orthodox Congregational Society of Walpole, and do adopt the following rules for the constitution of said society:

"1. Said society at their first meeting under this agreement shall elect one of the members as clerk, who shall record all the votes which are passed by the society.

"2. At the first meeting shall also be elected from among the members a standing committee of five in number, who shall have the management of all the concerns of the society according to the votes of said society.

"3. At the same meeting shall also be elected a committee of three whose duty it shall be to make certificates, for the purpose of giving notice according to law to the first society in Walpole, who are members of the society hereby formed.

"4. The society shall have the right to make all such by-laws, as they shall think fit to adopt from time to time, for the better carrying the purposes of the society into effect. Joshua Allen, Samuel Allen, Nathaniel P. Fisher, David Lewis, George P. Ellis, Henry Plimpton, William Lewis, Josiah Hill, Warren Wild, Jonathan Wild, Daniel Payson, Nathaniel Bird, Horatio Wood, Oliver Lincoln, Joseph Robbins, Sabin Ellis, Aaron Guild, Asa Fisher, Joel Fisher, William Fisher, Isaac Fisher, John Blackburn, Lewis Allen, Lewis Hartshorn, Liffe Smith, Mason Smith, Nathan Ware, Andrew Bird, Asa Hartshorn, George W. Kingsbury, John Morse, Thomas Frost, Jotham Morse, Jr., David Clap, John Hunt, Otis Clap, Lewis Clap, Amos Bardens, Harvey Ruggles, Daniel Ellis, Peter Smith, John Smith, Jr., Metcalf Smith, Wm. Kingsbury, Marcus Gilmore, Jacob Kingsbury, Ziba Baker, Willard Baker, Eli Bonney, Silas Fales, Moses Smith, Artemas Smith, Daniel Fisher, Benjamin N. Gay, Josiah Day, Lyman S. Ware, Charles Bonney, Warren Fales, Jason Clapp, Daniel Allen, Jason Lewis, Aaron Lewis, Jonathan Bird, Elijah Thompson, David Allen, Hermon Guild, Seth Clark, Josiah Hall, Joseph Guild, Eliphalet Ellis, Enoch Ellis Warren Fisher, John P. Bowker, Jerusha Clap, Rhoda Bird, Kesiah Kingsbery, Susan Lewis, Catherine Allen, Catherine Everett, Miriam Smith, Mercy Billings, Edward Brown.

The church, which was a part of and connected with the above society, was organized Nov. 13, 1826, by a council of ministers and delegates, at the house of Catherine Allen, situated at the corner of High Plain and Peach Street. Twenty-nine persons then and there assented to and signed the "Confession of Faith" and entered into "Covenant" with God and with each other: Herry Plimpton, Aaron Guild, Joshua Allen, Jonathan Wild, Rhoda Bird, Kesiah Thompson, Lucy Nason, Phebe Robbins, Nabby Robbins, Kesiah Kingsbury, Susanna Plimpton, Mercy Billings, Anna Ellis, Lucy Morse, Cynthia Guild, Priscilla Lewis, Catherine Everett, Sarah Smith, Catherine Allen, Mary Nason, Jerusha Clap,

Miriam Smith, Susanna Lewis, Milley Baker, Joanna Hill, Patty Bowker, Unity Allen.

For about a year this church worshiped in the old hall, so dear to old music lovers, the home of the old singing school, over Henry Allen's store, which stood some seventy-five feet back of the present Plimpton Block. There, until they could call a pastor, they were ministered unto by the Rev. Dr. Lyman Beecher, Rev. Mr. Burgess, Rev. Dr. Codman, and other eminent ministers of the orthodox faith.

A lot of land was soon after deeded to Daniel Allen, Sr., by Moses Fellt, Charlotte Wild, and Cushing Otis, on the easterly side of the road from Joshua Allen's house to Henry Allen's store. On this convenient but otherwise undesirable spot, after many sacrifices, at a cost of three thousand dollars, their first house of worship was erected, and in September, 1827, dedicated, the Rev. Dr. Codman preaching the sermon.

In 1837 the society voted that any persons connected with the society have the privilege to put a building on the society's land for a vestry, which led, soon after, to the building of a vestry beneath a part of the church, with its entrance door facing the street. This was used for prayer-meetings, singing schools, and other useful church work. The main door of the church was reached by a broad flight of steps erected in front of the building.

In 1850 the increased attendance made necessary the erection of galleries on three sides of the interior. The women and girls always occupied the eastern and the men and boys the western; even for some time men and

THE FIRST ORTHODOX CHURCH OF WALPOLE

Dedicated by Rev. Dr. Codman of Dorchester. The Rev. Asahel Bigelow Meeting-House on East Street, Walpole Centre

THE FIRST ORTHODOX PARSONAGE

Home of the Rev. Asahel Bigelow, on East Street, Walpole Centre. The parents of the writer, and many other original members of his society, were married in the lower right-hand front room

women arranged themselves on different sides of the vestry, as in the first Dedham churches. The front gallery was devoted to the choir and organ.

The first settled minister of this church was the Rev. Asahel Bigelow, like the minister of the mother church a graduate of Harvard College. He was installed March 12, 1828.

The society was still considered as belonging to the old parish and was for some time taxed for the support of the ministry there. Strong feeling was excited against the seceders, which did not die out until a very recent period and often caused great harm.

These taxes finally became so burdensome, payment was refused. The Rev. Mr. Bigelow peaceably paid his, but the Rev. Mr. Storer is said to have returned it.

There were, however, many that would not pay; so one of the offenders, Nathaniel P. Fisher, who lived on East Street just east of the place of Joshua Allen, was arrested. The members of this society under protest paid his tax, and brought suit for its recovery. The suit was decided in their favor, which put an end to the whole vexatious matter. The losing counsel was the Hon. Horace Mann, who in his argument referred to the new society as being only a few old women, which seemed too suggestive to the male portion to be relished.

In January, 1849, Mr. Bigelow removed to Hancock, N. H., where he labored for twenty years, and died at the ripe old age of eighty years.

The second pastor of this church was the Rev. George H. Newhall, a graduate of Amherst College in the class of 1845. He was installed Sept. 10, 1850. His ministry was notable but short, owing to feeble constitution and nervous temperament, but long enough to endear him to all with whom he came in contact. He died Aug. 24, 1853, at the age of twenty-seven years, and was buried in the burial lot of Deacon Everett Stetson in the Rural Cemetery.

The third pastor was the Rev. Edwin H. Nevin, who was installed Nov. 15, 1854. After a short pastorate, the general state of church affairs led to his dismissal by council to accept a call to the Plymouth Church, Chelsea, April 7, 1857.

For two years the pulpit of this church was supplied until choice was finally made of the Rev. Joseph W. Healey. He was installed Sept. 14, 1859, and remained in charge until 1862. He was then called to the Hanover Congregational Church of Milwaukee, Wis. He was so kind and anxious for the good of children, all now remember him with pleasure.

The Rev. Edward G. Thurber was the fifth pastor. He was ordained Oct. 29, 1862, and installed Oct. 14, 1863. He was active, earnest, and successful, but in 1870, after an exemplary ministry, removed to the Park Presbyterian Church, of Syracuse, N. Y., and has been until recently over the American Church in Paris, France.

The sixth pastor was the Rev. Hemon R. Timlow, of East Cambridge, who was installed Sept. 28, 1870, and dismissed by council July 26, 1872.

He was succeeded by Rev. Bela N. Seymour, who, after a year, was called to Ipswich, N. H.

E. Stetson

THE PRESENT ORTHODOX CHURCH, EAST STREET

The eighth pastor was the Rev. Henry L. Kendall, a bright and earnest preacher, but of feeble constitution. To him only thirty-four years were allowed in life's fitful journey. He was ordained Jan. 27, 1875. He removed to the First Congregational Church of Charlestown and then to Minneapolis. His remains now lie in the Maple Grove Cemetery.

The ninth pastor was the Rev. Calvin S. Hill, who was installed Sept. 27, 1876. He was courteous, kind, and able, and remained respected and loved by all until Aug. 1, 1881 when he removed to the First Congregational church of Milton.

The tenth pastor was Rev. Francis J. Marsh, Jan. 15, 1882. On the third Sabbath of March, 1893, after a long, eventful, and successful ministry, he tendered his resignation in order to enter upon the work of secretary of the Congregational Sabbath School and Publishing Society of Boston.

In October, 1894, the Rev. Frank C. Putnam was called to the pastorate, but soon removed to the old New Hampshire parish of his father.

Mr. Putnam was followed by the Rev. John L. Keedy, of Maryland, an earnest, industrious, and successful laborer in the Master's vineyard, but who is about to remove to the North Andover church. He does not go alone, however. One of his more desirable parishioners has decided to accompany him.

CHAPTER XI

AFTER the division of the old Walpole church, the Rev. Mr. Storer continued his ministry as usual, and all now can feel a personal interest and proper gratitude when we remember him as the founder of the beautiful elms that adorn what is now Common Street. Truly he was a public benefactor. His removal to take charge of an important church in Syracuse in 1839 was deeply deplored. He and the father of James Russell Lowell always remained true to Theodore Parker in his lonely days at West Roxbury and Boston.

Before the Rev. Mr. Storer removed, however, it was thought best to change the location of this church building. This building had been built under the supervision of Adam Blackman in 1783. After removing the eastern and western porches, it was swung round rear end first, guided by a pole stationed between the old and new sites, where it rests to-day, though much changed in both interior and exterior.

In August, 1839, the Rev. John M. Merrick received a call to become the Rev. Mr. Storer's successor, and, accepting, was installed the December 11th following. At the same time occurred the rededication of the renovated church building. The Rev. George Ripley, of

New Road to Wrentham   Site of first meeting-house and Meeting-House Common

WALPOLE COMMON   *Place of Rev. Mr. Storer*

Boston, preached the sermon to a crowded house. For twenty-six years Mr. Merrick patiently labored with this people, but in 1865 he resigned and removed to Charlestown, N. H., where he died March 20, 1871, leaving here a son, John M. Merrick, once well known as an analytical chemist.

The Rev. W. B. Smith, Mr. Merrick's successor, was installed Oct. 5, 1865, Dr. Hedge, of Brookline, preaching the sermon, and the Rev. Mr. Merrick making the address to the people.

During his ministry the galleries were taken down, a recess made back of the pulpit, and the pulpit lowered. At the reopening of the edifice, the Rev. Dr. Young, of the Harvard Divinity School, preached.

Mr. Smith, on account of a threatening malady, had gone to Europe for change and rest. From here he then sent his resignation. On returning home Mr. Smith, after preaching a few sermons, removed to Grafton, and the Rev. Mr. Young continued in charge.

Mr. Young was a scholarly man, of quiet and gentle manner, and well fitted for a select, intellectual, religious audience, but the members were few. He was never settled; probably because he would not consent.

The Rev. F. P. Hamblett succeeded, and was installed pastor March 22, 1877, Rev. J. F. Lovering preaching the sermon. He remained five years, and was greatly liked as a preacher and minister, although suffering from ill health. In 1882 he resigned, to retire to his old New Hampshire home, where he hoped to recover.

In November, 1882, the Rev. J. H. Weeks first preached

in this church, and continued upon a long and successful pastorate. Mr. Weeks was peculiarly well liked as a pastor by both old and young. He was also a talented artist and writer. He was followed by Rev. G. H. Clare 1891–1892, and Robert W. Savage, 1893–1901, and Rev Herman Haugerud 1902–1903.

The present pastor is the Rev. Joseph C. Allen, a young man full of promise, and earnestly desiring the highest welfare of the church and society.

Congregational Church of East Walpole. — For years Mr. F. O. Winslow and Sandford Waters Billings had perseveringly ministered to the spiritual wants of this part of the town. In April, 1877, a meeting was called at the house of Mrs. Seleny Smith for prayer, and to consult about celebrating the Lord's Supper. It was voted to request the Rev. C. B. Smith, who was settled over a small society in Dedham, to prepare a confession of faith and a covenant for the purpose of a church organization.

May 5 following, at another meeting held at the same place, it was voted to organize, and William Rhodes and Joseph Cheney were chosen deacons. On May 6 one person was baptized and eighteen joined in the celebration of the Lord's Supper. July 1, 1877, the Lord's Supper was again observed, and Ellen N. Brown, after baptism, admitted to the church.

Francis W. Bird had always generously offered the use of his small hall, on the condition, however, that all religious denominations should be equally welcomed. The Rev. Mr. Smith still continued to minister to them.

THE PRESENT UNITARIAN CHURCH, WALPOLE CENTRE, THE REV. MR. STORER'S CHURCH

HON. FRANCIS W. BIRD

Manufacturer and man eminent in affairs of the town and state

Sept. 3, 1877, William Rhoads, Samuel G. Fuller, and J. A. Brown were chosen to consider calling a council to recognize the church and recommend it to the fellowship of other churches.

On Oct. 18, 1880, an ecclesiastical council assembled at Bird Hall, of which Rev. C. G. Hill, of the Walpole church, was chosen moderator and Rev. Mr. Weston scribe. The churches of Walpole, Sharon, Norwood, Dedham, and Revere sent delegates, who voted to recognize and recommend the church. April 20, 1881, the church was admitted to full membership in the Massachusetts Suffolk South Conference.

June 6, 1882, at a meeting held at the house of William Rhodes, it was voted to erect a church building. For over a hundred years many of the families in this part of the town had worshiped with the church in South Dedham, beginning in 1732, and some had not yet parted with their legal rights there. William Rhodes, Mr. and Mrs. Samuel G. Fuller, and Simon Gould were chosen trustees, and the latter treasurer, of the new society.

On Oct. 14, 1882, Deacon William Rhodes presented them sufficient land on the southerly side of Union Street for their proposed new church building. This was built, and dedicated May 18, 1883, at which the Rev. A. H. Plumb, of Boston, preached the sermon. The cost of the building was about two thousand dollars. The Rev. Mr. Smith and the Rev. Mr. Bickford for years supplied the pulpit.

The Rev. Mr. Perkins, a faithful and popular pastor, for some years officiated as pastor. The Rev. John L.

Keedy has of late, in connection with his church in the Centre, ministered to their spiritual wants.

Methodist Episcopal Church, South Walpole.—In 1818, the Rev. Benjamin Haines came to this part of the town and introduced the doctrine of Methodism. Mr. Eliphalet Smith opened his house to the newcomer, and there the first meetings were held. The next year, Rev. Isaac Jennison, of Mansfield, formed here a class.

In 1822 Josiah Hall and others organized a church, and for thirty-five years thereafter Mr. Hall remained one of its chief officers. Its first pastor was the Rev. Francis Dane. There was no church building until 1830. It was built on the site of the parsonage given by Silas Smith. The Rev. Lewis Bates preached at its dedication.

In 1846 a new church building at the cost of three thousand seven hundred dollars was erected during the pastorate of Rev. D. L. Winslow, and was dedicated by the Rev. Dr. Charles Adams. Josiah Hall, Silas Smith, Caleb S. Ellis, R. Clap, J. Boyden, A. Ellis, and M. Smith were chosen trustees.

At a revival in 1834 this church received many valuable additions, notably Luman Boyden and Willard Smith, who afterward became useful ministers of the gospel. The church is usually supplied, but is in a fairly prosperous condition.

The Methodist Episcopal Church of Walpole Centre.—For years Mr. and Mrs. N. B. Winslow, in the north part of the town, had labored zealously in the cause of Methodism, and not without due results. After many sacrifices

THE METHODIST CHURCH, SOUTH WALPOLE

On the site of the first Methodist parsonage

and much labor a church was formed in the Centre, with a membership of twelve, of which the Rev. Mr. Noon was the first minister. He was followed by the Rev. J. H. Vincent, who is pleasantly remembered. Following him came Rev. H. V. Webster, Rev. E. Comstock, Rev. E. C. Farwell, one year each, the earnest Rev. F. O. Holman two years; Rev. M. D. Hornbeck, one year; the Rev. A. A. Kidder, one year; and others. The pulpit is always supplied by the conference, which has usually sent useful and able young men, largely students in the Boston University Divinity School.

For years Nathan W. Fisher has been its secretary and treasurer, and by earnest and self-sacrificing labor has kept the church together and at last secured a church building on the site of the old two-storied Centre school, which is an ornament to the centre of the town and an important factor in the religious advancement of the entire public.

St. Francis Catholic Church. — The largest and one of the more prosperous churches and religious socities in Walpole, at present, is the St. Francis Catholic. They have outgrown their present building and are planning one more commodious and satisfactory.

Fifty years ago the very few Catholic communicants here were wont to walk, like our early settlers, to Dedham town to worship. After many attempts, by holding public fairs, they at last became able to erect the present church building on East and Diamond streets.

For years the Rev. Francis Gouesse, who had received his education in Paris, France, ministered to the spiritual wants of the parish and, at his death, left it in a thriving condition.

The Rev. D. H. Riley, now officiating in his place, has greatly added to both the moral and spiritual well-being of all in the parish. Young, manly, and strong, much permanent good cannot but result from his earnest labor.

St. Mark's Episcopal Church. — The latest accession to the churches of the town is the St. Mark's Episcopal, soon to be re-dedicated. Its present rector, the Rev. Albert E. George, was the first to successfully gather the small flock and start it on its present course.

Upon his removal some years ago to his South Boston parish, the Rev. Samuel Lewis perseveringly ministered to the people. Bishop Phillips Brooks, so popular and dear to all religious sects, blessed also this church by his timely presence. A church building, after a period of worship in Bacon Hall, was erected on the corner of Common and West streets, during the pastorate of Rev. Wm. T. Dakin, and upon the return of the Rev. Mr. George to his old pastorate, a prosperous and useful life now seems to be again assured.

Town Hall. — For many years the common place of meeting, both in church and town affairs, was, as its name clearly implies, the Meeting-house; and even down to the year 1881 it so continued, the vestry of the First Church being then in use for that purpose. This vestry was low studded and ill ventilated, and at a crowded town meeting reeked with moisture and foul air, and was disliked and avoided in spite of town-meeting cake in the form of long sheets of nutmeg buns.

FANNY S. SCUDDER (NÉE FANNY S. LEWIS)

School-teacher, and for eighteen years missionary to India

Selectmen's Room *Cannon* *Former Library*

WALPOLE TOWN HALL

After enduring these conditions as long as they possibly could, several public-spirited citizens resolved to secure an appropriation for a modern town house. They did not stop to consider or imagine the other difficulties in the way. There soon sprang up a warmly expressed difference of opinion about both its location and its style of architecture, but finally the present brick structure was erected on a site a part of which had been purchased for the Methodist church.

On Sept. 25, 1881, the present building was dedicated. George E. Craig was chairman of the building committee, and on that occasion transferred the keys of the building into the hands of James G. Scott, chairman of the Board of Selectmen.

Mr. Craig had prepared his part and easily read it to the crowded audience, but the chairman of the selectmen, who had for years been so eloquent in holding office, was utterly unable to say a word. He finally accepted the keys, however.

Francis W. Bird, also, could find only a very few but pertinent words to say. Schoolmaster Hyde was called upon as an old Walpole boy. Edwin Thompson made one of his characteristic short speeches, but the most and better part of the services was an address by our worthy Walpole boy, Henry E. Fales, who was at his best. He has long since gone to his reward, but his work on that occasion still lives.

Many an address has followed from that platform. It is hoped that they have been fully as useful and inspiriting; and on the one hundred and sixty-eighth anniversary of the town, moved by the general ignorance of his fellow-townsmen concerning its notable namesake, another son, in the same earnest manner, on the presentation of an oil portrait, tried to arouse a proper interest in both Sir Robert Walpole and Rev. Phillips Payson. It bore fruit then. May it ever grow in fruitfulness. Two other notable gifts from other Walpole men have since followed: a useful and attractive band stand by Joseph J. Feeley, and an elaborate and much needed drinking fountain by George A. Plimpton. May they be appreciated. All gifts mean self-sacrifice and spring from a noble nature. The coarse way of regarding public gifts as merely vain displays of an overfilled purse is alike simple and vicious, and can never be tolerated by a decent community.

The Public Library. — More than thirty years ago a few of the more studious and progressive families in the east part of Walpole gathered together a considerable number of volumes, such as were commonly read at that period, and set out on a modest career of moral and intellectual education.

This was not the first worthy and successful undertaking of that nature in Walpole, however. The old Walpole Social Library of 1825, comprising the following members, has that honor, although on the separation of the orthodox society it resolved itself into a general historical society.

Others than these, who joined later, such as the Rev. J. P. B. Storer, should be added to the following; there were but few new members. Asa Allen, Lewis Allen,

WALPOLE PUBLIC LIBRARY

Corner of Lewis Avenue and Common Street, Walpole Centre

Nathaniel Bird, Eli Bonney, Leemon Boyden, Newell Boyden, George Bullard, Ebenezer W. Califf, Harvey Clap, Warren Clap, Ellis Clap, Levi Clap, Maynard B. Clap, Curtis Clap, Metcalf Clap, Truman Clarke, Francis Cole, Daniel Ellis, George P. Ellis, Jason Ellis, Hartford Ellis, Jesse Fairbanks, Squire M. Fales, Asa Fisher, Wilbur Gay, John Gilbert, Henry Goff, John A. Gould, Alvin Guild, Brayton Hartshorn, Willard Hartshorn, Asa Hartshorn, Joseph Hartshorn, Catherine Hartshorn, Richard Hartshorn, Ebenezer Hartshorn, Otis Hartshorn, Joseph Hawes, Isaac Hunt, John Hunt, Fisher A. Kingsbury, Harlow Lawrence, William Lewis, George H. Mann, Sally Messinger, Palmer Morey, Daniel Payson, Nathaniel Polley, Jr., Ephraim Shepard, Joshua Stetson, Jr., Everett Stetson, Ebenezer Stone, Daniel Turner, Jonathan Ware, Asa Whitman, Warren Wild, Roland Willett, Horatio Wood. The writer has some of its volumes still, notably "Plutarch's Lives."

However, the library at East Walpole was the mother of our present efficient town library. It was offered to the town, and the town, for a beginning, was glad to possess even the poor fiction it contained. One of the conditions of the gift was that its literary treasures, for a term of years, should be delivered free to our East Walpole citizens. This was faithfully kept. The new library the town first placed, with some few additions, in the southwest corner room of the town hall, and soon extended its healthy influence to all parts of the town.

Many years have passed since then, but its growth has increased, and, it is hoped, its influence for good in the same proportion, until the town hall location grew entirely inadequate for its accommodation.

Francis W. Bird, ever a true friend to progress, mindful of the faithful and beneficent life of his daughter, Mary R. Bird, left by his will a legacy of $3,000 for a library building. This encouraged certain citizens, not realizing the demoralizing effect of their hasty and ill-considered project, to secure a new building in the quickest possible way. The great public benefactor in libraries both here and abroad, Andrew Carnegie, was approached for assistance. He offered the town $15,000 on the condition that $1,500 should be annually appropriated for the library's support. By persevering labor, enough more was secured to erect the present new building on Common Street. The success of the undertaking was materially advanced by a timely gift of the site by Mr. Bird's son, Charles Sumner Bird. It was a beautiful offering, and should have been followed by such a public-spirited response that the town would have been spared the humiliating and pauperizing experience of begging assistance from an entire stranger.

The Walpole Woman's Club, and the Wednesday Club. — Even the briefest history should not omit woman's helpful assistance in moral and religious education and achievements. The patient, whole-souled mother of the past, the child-loving, burden-bearing wife of our youth, is being fast supplanted by a far different order of woman, who strives to emulate man in all his varied activities. Hence the "club," whose only justification can be in the great possibilities for general good. In 1895 the Walpole

MARY R. BIRD

Faithful co-worker for the Public Schools and Town Library

A TYPICAL, MODEL WIFE AND MOTHER OF THE LAST CENTURY, IN HER EIGHTY-FOURTH YEAR

Woman's Club was formed at the centre of the town, with Martha M. Allen president, and Harriet R. Gray vice-president. In 1900 Mrs. Allen was succeeded by Helen M. Way, who was followed by Minnie Merrick in 1902, and Annie M. Stowell in 1903. In several fields of general work much good has been accomplished, particularly in the schools and a general increased sociability among the different religious bodies. Scoffing at the good and true is now confined to a very insignificant few. Like a church, by avoiding the weaknesses of its officers, a whole society can rise to higher levels and much other good be accomplished.

The Wednesday Club of the east part of the town, as old and helpful as its sister society in the Centre, has always been under the presidency of Anna C. Bird, who in many ways has filled the place of her unselfish sister-in-law, Mary R. Bird of pleasant memory. This club has the advantage of a club-house, well appointed and convenient to both electric and steam roads. Between one and two thousand dollars are annually appropriated by this club, between its good intentions and actual accomplishments. Clubs, like cities and towns, never get full value or credit for either time or money, and for this reason, if for no other, the utmost care should be taken in the selection of objects for special work. No village of its size can boast of better equipment or greater achievements than this well-known club. In a place where originated our Public Library, the High School, and open advocacy of universal freedom, it has every incentive to lead in every good and useful work.

The Norfolk, Plymouth and Bristol County Truant School. — Soon after the close of the Civil War, Joel and Olive Lewis Fales erected a large and attractive dwelling-house on their land, on the summit of the old training ground and powder depository known as Powder House Hill, located near the centre of the town. Both had ample means, and the uncommon beauty and attractiveness of the site justified the notable buildings they planned for their permanent future home. Never possessing robust health, in spite of travel and recreation for physical benefit, both husband and wife rapidly sank to their graves. The beautiful home, not long after, became a part of the sanitarium field of Dr. Cullis, of Grove Hall, Boston. Upon his death, the county commissioners of Norfolk, Plymouth, and Bristol counties, in need of some convenient place for carrying into effect new legal requirements concerning persistent and incorrigible truant scholars, secured the premises and immediately made improvements necessary for their future purposes. Here many boys, and a few girls, have since found wise and helpful training and discipline to upbuild and strengthen against natural waywardness. The superintendents and teachers have always been equal to the great task officially imposed upon them and have generally received due encouragement and respect from the people of the town.

Joel Fales, the original owner of the premises, in connection with his father-in-law, Deacon Willard Lewis, invented many useful mechanical devices for the latter's manufactures. His brother, Charles Fales, soon entered the employ of Mr. Lewis, and at his death left a son,

Lewis F. Fales, who now, in emulation of his predecessors, is still conducting one of the most important branches of Walpole's many and varied manufactures, that of constructing and designing intricate and useful machinery. From Eleazer Smith's card and nail and Ira Gill's hat machinery to the daily product of this shop is a long step, but the public can well feel proud of both old and new Walpole achievements.

There are many things that might well be added to a historic volume of fully as much interest as anything in the foregoing pages, — biography, genealogy and anecdote, — but both time and space prevent.

The town has always been blessed by abundant water power, and means of transportation. The Neponset River and its tributaries, and ever since the completion of the old Norfolk County steam railroad, its successor, the Boston, Hartford & Erie, the New York & New England, and now the New York, New Haven & Hartford, have all fostered our manufactures The advent of electric roads has also been a constantly increasing public advantage.

In earlier days, we had the old-time stage-coach and four on three of our principal throughfares, and the two old buildings, Fuller and Polley taverns, on opposite sides of Washington Street in the south part of the town, bravely testify both to the importance of stage-coach travel and their own great usefulness. The old Roeback Tavern, where Lafayette once was entertained, on the corner of the old Post Road and Coney Street in the east part of the town, also deserves attention. Even the old milestone erected by Ezekiel Robbins, the keeper of the old Brass Ball Tavern near the Lewis batting mills, which thirty years ago stood west of Powder House Hill on the road to the Plain (once a coach road, with John Needham's old tavern this side of the Horace Guild house,) but now removed to the town hall, is eloquent with interest. Who now remembers John Needham, or that he carried on his stages free all that would leave his rival?

Manufactures. — Long before this part of Dedham was settled, a grant was made to Eleazer Lusher and Joshua Fisher to build and operate a sawmill here, near the Great Cedar Swamp, that has, already, been minutely referred to. It, like most of the industries of Walpole, was on or near the Neponset River. This was followed by the sawmill of Ebenezer Fales on what is now Spring Brook, and Mr. Morse on Stop River. On the first map of Walpole, that of 1794, there is represented a sawmill at Blackburn's, and a grist-mill at Stetson's.

Neponset River, from its source to the mill of Hollingsworth and Vose in the east part of the town, has the combined fall of one hundred and fifty-one feet.

Beginning in the south part of the town, the fall at the old Elbridge Smith pond is fourteen feet. Timothy Gay, of Dedham, operated a grist-mill there, in old coach-running days of 1814. Besides grinding grain, he acted as toll-gate keeper at a gate near his mill. Here Daniel and Elbridge Smith afterwards built a mill for the manufacture of cotton goods. Here, also, Sumner, of Canton, afterwards made rubber lining, and Bradford Lewis made cotton from clippings.

The next privilege on the river was that of Henry S. Clarke, and has a fall of twenty-one feet. In 1750 Theodore Mann manufactured cloth here, as also did his son Col. Timothy Mann, and his grandson Timothy Mann. In 1812 there were two distinct privileges here. Col. Mann, clothier, occupied the lower; James Richardson & Co. made nails at the upper. The Boston and Walpole Manufacturing Co., of which the Hon. Truman Clarke was agent here, afterwards carried on the same business. Upper Mill was rebuilt by Eli Bonney, Leavitt Kingsbury, and David Ruggles. In 1820 broadcloths and cassimeres were here manufactured by Howe & Richardson. The Hon. Truman Clarke, having married a daughter of Timothy Mann, came into possession of the mill, and for years used it for the manufacture of woolen goods, broadcloths, and cassimeres. The lower mill, after burning, was never rebuilt. In 1836 John Mann began here to manufacture boots and shoes, and joined Mr. Clarke in the partnership of Clarke & Mann. They bought and converted the old Boston & Providence Coach Company's stable, part into a shoe shop, part into a dwelling-house. The business is said to have been one hundred and fifty thousand dollars a year.

Afterwards, in 1851, Mr. Clarke's son, Henry S. Clarke, united with Naaman Wilmarth, and made stocking yarn here. Mr. Wilmarth retiring from the business in 1862, it was continued by Mr. Clarke until his death in 1881. His son W. H. Clarke has, at times, since run the mill, but on the advent of the Norfolk Electric Street Railroad Company sold the building for their future use in railroading.

The old Rucaduc privilege next follows. It has a fall of twelve feet. It, previous to 1812, was a part of the William Bacon farm. Mr. Bacon afterwards joined with Horace and Eliphalet Smith and Horace Clap, and in 1812 ran a sawmill, shingle mill, and carding machine mill there. Mr. Bacon wanted to irrigate a portion of his land, and his partner Smith is said to have called the reservoir or aqueduct thus made a "rucaduc"; hence its old name. Daniel and Elbridge Smith afterwards purchased the privilege, and erected a cotton mill for the manufacture of cotton thread. Mr. Jenks, William H. Cary, James Ogden, and the Walpole emery mill have all since occupied this privilege.

Then comes the old Blackburn privilege, with a seven-foot fall, where Aaron Blake built his dam and sawmill, and used the right to flow the stream. In 1816 it had gone into the hands of Samuel Nason and John Boyden. Besides the sawmill, they operated a grist-mill just below, where the fall was twelve feet.

June 11, 1811, these privileges were purchased by John Blackburn, of Medway, who began the manufacture of machinery, and in the upper part of the building George Blackburn and his father John Blackburn manufactured cotton yarn, until the building was destroyed by fire. George afterwards owned factories in Mansfield, Ashland, and Fitchburg. In 1846 John Henry Blackburn, having united with Ollis Clap, and having bought the foundry of Everett Stetson at Stetson's pond, removed the tools and other personal property to his father's lower privilege, and began the casting of stoves, fire frames, and machinery.

Afterwards J. H. Blackburn, giving up the foundry, began making shingles and grinding grist at the same place. Asa Whitman and Ephraim Shepard both occupied a part of one of the old mills, one for lamp wicks, the other for carriages.

The fifth privilege, that of the old Union Factory, now the Massachusetts Chemical Co. mill, has a fall of eighteen and a half feet. Here to 1812 Samuel Fales manufactured snuff. Here Thaddeus Clap and Samuel Fuller had a tan yard. Daniel Ellis manufactured cloth. Eliphalet Clap had a forge for iron and nails.

In 1813 Oliver Clap, Daniel Ellis, Warren Clap, Daniel Payson, called Oliver Clap & Co., having bought the land of Ebenezer Clap and the right to convey the water through his land, became the Walpole Union Manufacturing Company; Oliver Clap, president, Warren Clap, treasurer, Oliver Eldredge, clerk. Asa Whitman was one of its agents.

On Dec, 15, 1849, the property came into the hands of Smith Gray, James S. Shepard, and William H. Cary, who, a few years later, conveyed it to Charles Manning, Henry R. Glover, and Jerome B. Cram under the name of Manning, Glover & Co., manufacturers of curled hair mattresses, cotton batting, and wicking until 1872. Mr. Cram continued the business until 1880, but then sold to Smith Gerrish. Stephen Pember afterwards leased the premises, but a fire soon swept away all the buildings. The privilege has, for some years, been in the hands of the Massachusetts Chemical Company, who also own the two old Blackburn privileges above.

The sixth old privilege has a nine-foot fall, and was owned in 1812 by Daniel Clap, who had here manufactured cloth for many years. In 1821 an old employee of the mill above came into possession of the water power and erected a new mill, with the customary bell tower, and continued until his death the manufacture of cotton thread. His heirs, for some ten years after, under the care of Capt. George Guild, further continued the business. This old employee was Harlow Lawrence.

Feb. 21, 1863, Deacon Willard Lewis, who had been engaged in the manufacture of listing carpets and lint bandages for the U. S. Government, in the old disused schoolhouse and an adjoining building in the east part of the town, purchased of the heirs of Mr. Lawrence the whole property, and, in addition to the lint business, afterwards carried on the manufacture of carpet lining, cotton batting, and cotton percolator used in the Southern States for straining rosin. William Hart had there a small machine shop. A disastrous fire destroyed both the old buildings and obliged Mr. Lewis to rebuild, which he at once did, erecting a brick building of considerable proportions. After his death his son W. I. Lewis continued the business until he sold to George A. Plimpton the whole plant, which is now run under the name of the Lewis Batting Company.

Deacon Bradford Lewis & Son occupy the mill site below in the manufacturing of cardboard and cotton waste.

The next privilege is commonly called Stetson's, and has a fall of twelve feet. At the time of the Revolutionary War there was a grist-mill here owned mostly by Gay and Cleaveland, which several times changed hands till about 1794 it came into the possession of Ebenezer Hartshorn. John Cleaveland, John Hooper, an old Crown Point soldier, and Jeremiah and Samuel Dexter, from the Crown Point expedition to the War of the Revolution, had a forge near. In 1796 Joshua Stetson, who had wandered this way from what is now Randolph, purchased this privilege, having at times both a forge for the manufacture of hoes and other agricultural tools, and a foundry for stoves, fire frames, and other cast-iron articles. He learned his trade at Randall's in Sharon, and is said to have made an agreement with the Ameses and others not to manufacture axes, ploughs, and shovels, or such articles as formed a competition. Deacon Henry Plimpton was at one time with him. His goods held the highest place in the market. In 1827 he is said to have given up his business to his son Everett, who continued this business until 1830.

The father died in 1863. His son Joshua Stetson, Jr., in 1830 began here the manufacture of cotton goods, which, with varied success, he continued down to 1867. His ticking, like his father's hoes, was the best the market afforded. In 1855, having some years before sold his foundry to Blackburn & Clapp, Deacon Everett Stetson purchased the entire property and removed the factory in which he had for some time manufactured card clothing to its present position.

In 1867 his son Edward assumed the card-clothing business, but having several years ago joined the American Card Clothing Company, the factory, until quite recently, has been more or less in disuse. It is now used by the Walpole Card Clothing Company.

This spot is memorable as the field of labor of the ingenious but improvident inventor Eleazer Smith. It has always been claimed that the fruits of this man's ingenuity in producing the card-clothing machine were deliberately stolen from him here. He was also the inventor of a nail cutting or making machine and a match machine from which he profited nothing. He is said to have lived on High Street, and that his remains rested unmarked in the Rural Cemetery until the widows of Deacon Everett Stetson and Joshua Stetson, Jr., just prior to their deaths, kindly erected the present tablet.

At this old privilege for years labored another great genius, Ira Gill, the hat manufacturer. Chauncey Smith, one of our most famous patent solicitors, once declared to the writer that Mr. Gill was one of the most ingenious men of the age. In 1823 Mr. Gill began near here the manufacture of fur-napped hats. He later took up fur felt goods. Mr. Roberts had many years before manufactured hats, but was succeeded by Rand & Hooper, who were Mr. Gill's immediate predecessors.

Who has attended the old town meetings in the Unitarian vestry and does not remember Ira Gill? He could not be forgotten, if one would, that old watch-dog of the town treasury and scoffer at reform. On one occasion, observing the harsh criticism and no little abuse of our most noted fellow townsman, Francis W. Bird, and recognizing that a little less regard to conscience could easily make Mr. Bird's daily path more easy, he once

CALVIN G. PLIMPTON

Senior member of C. G. & H. M. Plimpton, who down to the War of the Rebellion furnished much of the iron supplies for the development of our great far West, and the axle-skins for the overland prairie schooner

exclaimed, "Frank Bird, you are a fool. What do you care about things way down South? Slavery don't harm us up here, does it? Yes, you are a darned, plaguey old fool."

It is needless to say that Mr. Bird changed not his opinion. He himself, but a few days before, characterized Joseph Billings of West Roxbury pretty much in the same way, when Billings refused to fall into line with the then new Republican movement.

The next privilege, taking both ponds together, has a fall of eighteen and a half feet. Here, in 1810, John Stanley and Dr. Thomas Stanley, manufactured tacks and snuff, the Stanleys selling in 1811 to Virgil Maxey, counsellor at law. William Appleton afterwards came and purchased the old Lewis Lane and Hartshorn road, thus being the first owner of all what is now called Plimpton Street. Maxey was from Baltimore, Maryland; the Stanleys from Attleboro. They are not known as owners of anything but the lower privilege. The land was originally a part of the farm of Roland Willet.

In 1816 Henry Plimpton began to occupy the upper privilege, largely in the manufacture of hoes. A foundry was afterwards added. In 1844 Deacon Henry Plimpton purchased the lower Ellis privilege. He was succeeded by his two sons, Calvin G. and H. M. Plimpton, who in 1848 formed a copartnership as C. G. & H. M. Plimpton, who continued the manufacture of hoes, springs, axles, and other iron goods until 1865, when, the elder partner having died, the property was sold to Boston parties called the Linden Spring and Axle Company, of which

Hubbard W. Tilton was president, and Gen. William Tilton treasurer with Boston men as directors. Almost all the buildings disappeared, one after another, by fire, until now only the old carpenter shop remains. The property now belongs to George A. Plimpton, one of the sons of C. G. Plimpton referred to.

This lower privilege was for years known as the Ellis privilege, from Daniel Ellis, who in 1818, with his son George, here manufactured satinet goods. In 1835 the father died, leaving his son to continue the business to 1837. He was succeeded by George Blackburn for four years. Negro cloth was afterwards made here by Mr. Freeman. He was succeeded by Calvin Turner. His successors, Park Stearns and Blackburn, then in 1844 sold to Deacon Henry Plimpton, who made hosiery yarn and satinets for a short time. Oliver W. Allen & Co., Henry Plimpton, Oliver W. Allen and Jeremiah Allen, later manufactured twine here, and Everett Stetson wadding.

The next privilege, that of F. W. Bird & Son, has a fall of fifteen feet. In early times, before 1818, Eliphalet Rhoads had a small grist-mill here, with a narrow lane leading out to the street beyond. He occupied a little red house under the hill above the mill, to the south. He sold the privilege and a good deal of adjoining land on the northeast to one Webb, who built a cotton mill and the long tenement house for a generation known as the Webb house, where now stands the freight house of the N. Y., N. H. & H. R.R.

Rhoads was obliged to take back the property and, not wanting it himself, gladly sold to Dean, Sayles &

Co., who continued there the manufacture of cotton cloth, under the name of the Neponset Manufacturing Company. They built a new dam and purchased flowage rights, absorbing the old rights and dam which George Bird, the father of Francis W. Bird, had just purchased to control the owners below, between this privilege and that of the Ellis dam above.

In 1835 this company sold to Silas Smith, Jabez Coney and others, who, under the name of the Neponset Paper Mill Company, began the manufacture of printing paper.

This company, for the purpose of closing their business, sold to one of their members, Jabez Coney, who in 1838 sold to Francis W. Bird.

Mr. Bird at first manufactured news printing paper, but soon gave it up for the more profitable coarser wrapping paper goods for screws, provisions, and groceries. Here, during the whole after public life of Mr. Bird, with but few reverses, was conducted a business so liberal to employees that it would now be impossible either to understand or follow it. Manila papers, box papers, cartridge papers, waterproof and roofing papers have here, under the management of Charles S. Bird, superseded the general class of goods at first manufactured.

In the near-by memorial tower to Mr. Bird is a Paul Revere bell and Howard clock, a gift from the neighboring citizens.

The last water privilege, that of Hollingsworth & Vose, has a twelve-foot water fall. The father of Francis W. Bird, George Bird, came here from East Dedham somewhere about 1817 and began the manufacture of paper as

Bird & Son, having his son Josiah N. Bird with him. For some years the son ran it alone, but in 1833 sold out to his brother Francis W. Bird. Thomas W. Kennedy, Bird & Presby and others manufactured paper here until 1882, when Francis W. Bird sold the privilege to Mr. Z. Hollingsworth, who took into partnership Charles Vose, under the firm name of Hollingsworth & Vose. For many years a prosperous paper business has been here conducted. Mr. Vose has lately built for himself a spacious home in one of the most beautiful spots in town and is now regarded a permanent fellow townsman.

Upon Spice or Spring Brook there was early one or more sawmills, the most notable one being that of Deacon Ebenezer Fales. At the Diamond Pond there is a fifteen-foot fall. In 1814 Dr. Jonathan Wilde and wife sold this privilege to Samuel Hartshorn and Daniel Kingsbury. A company was formed to operate it. Among them were Ebenezer Hartshorn, Daniel Kingsbury, Nathaniel Guild, Josiah Hill, Hermon Guild, Samuel Allen, James Guild, and Robert Robertson, with Daniel Kingsbury as agent. For several years they manufactured cotton goods. In 1868 Hartshorn & Kingsbury conducted the same business here, and afterwards hemp twine.

In 1829 the Diamond Manufacturing Company with twenty-four shares was incorporated and began manufacturing here. Daniel Carpenter, of Foxboro, sold his twelve shares to Smith Gray. In 1842 Asa Whitman deeded to his son Henry C. Whitman, who in turn sold to Smith Gray in 1844. Gray leased it to Joshua Stetson, Jr., and William Bullard.

DEACON JEREMIAH ALLEN

DEACON WILLARD LEWIS

In 1858 Simeon Clap, who had from 1842 to 1850 been a manufacturer of straw goods, became its owner, when he began the manufacture of stocking yarns, Java canvas and twine thread. In 1881, upon the death of Mr. Clap, it was sold to Deacon Bradford Lewis for curing wool, who afterwards sold to John B. Rooney, who is still in business there.

Above the latter privilege was early a machine shop kept by Royal Smith, who lived near. He also manufactured cotton and woolen machinery here. It was, however, destroyed by fire in 1860.

In 1880 Nathan Clark and his son Alton came into possession, rebuilt the dam, and erected a sawmill. This was afterward sold to H. A. Morse & Co., who conduct a large lumber business there, Mr. Clark going still farther up stream.

Among other early town industries, the early straw works of Samuel Gilbert is perhaps the best known, situated a little away from his residence, to the east of the Orthodox church. Farther back, Ephraim Shepard, who lived where Horace A. Spear now lives, made furniture, carriage supplies, and even coffins. Josiah Hill also manufactured furniture near the new house of John P. O'Brion. Horace Guild also had a furniture shop on Walpole Plain; so also did Deacon Nathaniel Bird and his brother.

In 1832 Deacon Jeremiah Allen began the manufacture of twine and fish lines near his home on Peach Street, carrying occasionally by horse to Boston a few samples for trade. His goods were prized everywhere.

His honesty and conscientiousness produced for the trade a perfect article. At the Philadelphia Centennial his goods received the first and highest premium and honor. In 1866 he took into partnership Samuel Allen, who for years had been clerk for C. G. & H. M. Plimpton, and another shop was at once added. Both partners have long gone to their reward, that of good citizens and honest business men. Horace Plimpton and John W. Blackburn were at one time large manufacturers of hoop skirts.

The Smith Gray Company, now a corporation of which Robert S. Gray is president, which does a large and select dyeing and bleaching business, is but the successor of Mr. Gray's father, the well-known Smith Gray, who at one time did a large and profitable business in the same line at the same location.

In 1825 Squire M. Fales carried on a foundry above Walpole Plain, which was afterwards purchased by General Leach of Easton, who continued until 1845 in puddling iron and the manufacture of iron goods from iron ore, much of which came from near Spring Brook. Thomas and George Campbell, in 1845, purchased the mill and began the manufacture of paper.

Mr. John P. Bowker also was a manufacturer of straw goods. The Mahoney Mattress Company does a large business in furniture and mattresses.

The Morey privilege on Mill Brook, having a fall of sixteen feet, is still in use. Here for years was a prosperous sawmill. In 1840 Lewis W. Robbins and Erastus Robbins manufactured carriage axles here until 1853.

The brother having died, Lewis W. Robbins continued alone until 1855. In 1854 George Morey, brother of Palmer Morey, purchased the property and transferred it in 1863 to his brother, who in 1868 transferred it to his son George P. Morey.

Henry D. Dupee, some years ago, established over opposite the Walpole railroad station the business of manufacturing dyes, under the name of Dupee, Weeks & Soren. It is now operated by Mr. Alfred Smith.

The American Furniture Company a few years ago carried on an extensive business in school furniture diagonally opposite the factory of Henry D. Dupee. Some business is still carried on there, but to less extent than formerly.

List of Representatives to General Court. — There was no representative previous to 1740, and although subject to a fine, for years the town continuously voted not to choose one. In 1768 Joshua Clap was chosen; in 1769, Seth Kingsbury; from 1770 to 1772, Joshua Clap; Enoch Ellis in 1773; in the Provincial Congress, Enoch Ellis represented the town in 1774; Enoch Ellis was chosen in 1775 to represent the town for six months at the Congress at Watertown; July 16, 1775, Benjamin Kingsbury was chosen to represent the town at the Great and General Court at Watertown; Joshua Clap was chosen representative in 1776; Benjamin Kingsbury in 1777; Seth Bullard from 1778 to 1780 inclusive; from 1781 to 1783, there was no choice of representative; Seth Bullard from 1754 to 1786; Enoch Ellis, 1787; Seth Kingsbury, 1788; Shubael Downs, 1789; Seth Bullard, 1790; in 1791 and

1792 no choice; Oliver Clap, 1793 to 1795 inclusive; Seth Bullard from 1796 to 1798; Moses Ellis, 1799; Seth Bullard, 1800; William Bacon, 1801; Oliver Clap in 1802; William Bacon in 1803; Asa Kingsbury from 1804 to 1818 inclusive; Daniel Kingsbury in 1809 to 1816 inclusive; no representatives in 1817, 1818, 1819; Jesse Boyden in 1820; voted not to elect in 1822; Harvey Clap in 1823 to 1825 inclusive; voted not to choose in 1826; Joseph Hawes in 1827 to 1831 inclusive; Phineas Ellis, 1832; Truman Clarke, 1833, 1834; Joseph Hawes, 1835; Joshua Stetson, Jr., 1836, 1837, 1838; Emmons Partridge, 1839; Palmer Morey, 1840, 1841; Oliver W. Allen, 1842, 1843; George Bullard, 1844, 1845; Francis W. Bird, 1846, 1847; Rev. Asahel Bigelow, 1848, 1849; Palmer Morey, 1850, 1851: voted not to choose, 1852; Deacon Henry Plimpton, 1853; Harvey Boyden, 2d, 1854; Deacon Jeremiah Allen, 1855, 1856; In 1857 the Eleventh Representative District of Norfolk County was formed, including Milton, Sharon, Canton and Walpole, and no one was chosen from Walpole from 1857 to 1862; Elbridge Piper, 1862; Naaman B. Wilmarth, 1863; none in 1864; John M. Merrick, 1865; Francis W. Bird, 1866; none in 1867; Francis W. Bird, 1868; none in 1869, 1870, 1871; Willard Lewis, 1872, 1873; Samuel Allen, 1874; none in 1875; Francis W. Bird, 1876, 1877; Henry S. Clarke, 1878; none in 1879, 1880; George E. Craig, 1881, 1882. Since then a new district with Stoughton, Sharon, and Walpole has been formed, which has been represented by Robert S. Gray in 1889, 1890, and Joseph Leach.

Town Clerks of Walpole: Samuel Kingsbury, 1724-

1728; Ezra Morse, 1729; Samuel Kingsbury, 1730–1738; Joshua Fisher, 1739–1747; Aquilla Robbins, 1748–1767; Stephen Felch, 1768–1773; Seth Clap, 1774–1775; Benjamin Kingsbury, 1776; Seth Clap, 1777; George Payson, 1778; Stephen Felch, 1779–1799; Asa Kingsbury, 1800–1808; Samuel Hartshorn, 1809–1814; Harvey Clap, 1815–1832; Joshua Stetson, Jr., 1833–1844; Palmer Morey, 1845–1864; George P. Morey, 1865–1883; Henry E. Craig, Harry L. Howard.

The Common. — The first mention of the Common appears very early in 1663, when the Dedham minister is granted a few acres of land on a "Plain half a Mile this Side of the Saw Mille." At the same time the field, in which are now the Glover, Hartshorn, and Boyden houses, was known as the Major's Plain. The old Wrentham and the old Sawmill roads, both laid out before the first meeting-house was erected, met a little west of where the Walpole and Wrentham turnpike was afterward built. A good deal of what is now the west end of the Common was a part of the open field adjoining.

The original layout of the old Sawmill road was early carried westward from the Woodward field to that of William Robbins, Sr., because there was a bridge over Spice or Spring Brook at that point. After crossing the brook the road meandered up the hill, avoiding its high crown by turning to the south by the house of Thomas Clap. This hilltop remained to annoy the early settler until the second meeting-house was built. Thomas Clap gave the first meeting-house site to the town, or sold it, rather. It was a small piece, and after the first meeting-house was built thereon it began to be called the "Meeting House Common."

On the building of the second meeting-house, the hill was taken away and an addition made to the meeting-house grounds or "Common." The last addition was in 1828, and included over an acre. The donors were Warren Clap, yeoman; Harlow Lawrence, manufacturer; Ebenezer Stone, physician; Everett Stetson, blacksmith; Horatio Wood, carpenter; John Gilbert, yeoman; John P. B. Storer, clerk; Asa Whitman, manufacturer; Joseph Hawes, yeoman; Truman Clarke, manufacturer; Richard Hartshorn, yeoman; Nathaniel Bird, chairmaker; Joseph Ellis, yeoman; Daniel Kingsbury, Esq.; Harvey Clap, Esq.; Joshua Stetson, Jr., manufacturer. They then had laid out West Street and Elm Street, and had put the Walpole and Wrentham turnpike on the other side of the church, leveling over the old thoroughfare. This accounts for the seeming inconsistent location of the first two meeting-houses on early plans.

In order to guide the reader to a correct understanding of our early political action, the following paper has been thought of the highest importance:

GOVERNORS OF MASSACHUSETTS

CHOSEN ANNUALLY BY THE PEOPLE

Province of Massachusetts Bay under the first charter: 1629, Mar. 4, Matthew Cradock; 1629, Apr. 30, John Endicott; 1629, Oct. 20, John Winthrop; 1634, May 14, Thomas Dudley; 1635, May 6, John Haynes; 1636, May 25, Henry Vane; 1637, May 17, John Winthrop; 1640, May 13, Thomas Dudley; 1641, June 2, Richard Bellingham; 1642, May 18, John Winthrop; 1644, May 29, John Endicott; 1645, May 14, Thomas

Dudley; 1646, May 6, John Winthrop; 1649, May 2, John Endicott; 1650, May 22, Thomas Dudley; 1651, May 7, John Endicott; 1654, May 3, Richard Bellingham; 1655, May 23, John Endicott; 1665, May 3, Richard Bellingham; 1672, Dec. 12, John Leverett; 1673, May 7, John Leverett; 1679, May 28, Simon Bradstreet to 1686.

Plymouth Colony: 1620, Nov. 11, John Carver; 1621, April, William Bradford; 1633, Jan. 1, Edward Winslow; 1634, Mar. 27, Thomas Prince; 1635, Mar. 3, William Bradford; 1636, Mar. 1, Edward Winslow; 1637, Mar. 7, William Bradford; 1638, June 5, Thomas Prince; 1639, June 3, William Bradford; 1644, June 5, Edward Winslow; 1645, June 4, William Bradford; 1657, June 3, Thomas Prince; 1673, June 3, Josiah Winslow; 1680, Dec. 18, Thomas Hinckley.

May 25, 1686, Joseph Dudley assumed the office of President, under a commission from James II, and, with a Council, had jurisdiction over New England. He was superseded December 20 of the same year by Sir Edmund Andros who had been appointed by the same king. April 20, 1689, Governor Andros was deposed by popular revolution.

After the Dissolution of the First Charter, Simon Bradstreet from May 24, 1689, to May 14, 1692.

Appointed by the king under second charter: 1692, May 14, Sir William Phipps; 1694, Nov. 17, William Stoughton; 1699, May 26, Richard Coote Earl of Bellomont; 1700, July, William Stoughton; 1701, July 7, The Council; 1702, June 11, Joseph Dudley; 1714–15, Feb., the Council; 1715, Nov. 9, William Tailor; 1716, Oct. 4, Samuel Shute; 1722, Dec. 27, William Dummer; 1728, July 15, William Burnet; 1729, Sept. 7, William Dummer; 1730, June 30, William Tailor; 1730, Aug. 8, Jonathan Belcher; 1741, Aug. 17, William Shirley; 1749, Sept. 11, Spencer Phips; 1753, Aug. 7, William Shirley; 1756, Sept. 25, Spencer Phips; 1757, Aug. 3, Thomas Pownal; 1760, June 3, Thomas Hutchinson; 1761, Aug. 1, Sir Francis Bernard; 1769, Aug. 1, Thomas Hutchinson; 1771, March, Thomas Hutchinson; 1774, May 13, Thomas Gage.

Until the Constitution: 1774, Oct., Provincial Congress; 1775, July, the Council.

A Committee of Safety was appointed which, with the exception of appointment to office, performed the executive duties of the government. The act authorizing the election of the first Council provided that the Provincial Congress should consider the Constitutional Council of the province as governor of the province.

Under the Constitution: 1780 to 1785, John Hancock; 1785–1787, James Bowdoin; 1787–1793, Oct. 8, John Hancock; 1794–1797, Samuel Adams; 1797–1799, June 7, Increase Sumner; 1800–1807, Caleb Strong; 1807–1808, Dec. 10, James Sullivan; 1809–1810, Christopher Gore; 1810–1812, Elbridge Gerry; 1812–1816, Caleb Strong; 1816–1823, John Brooks; 1823–1825, Feb. 6, John Eustis; 1825–1834, Levi Lincoln; 1834–1835, Mar. 1, John Davis; 1836–1840, Edward Everett; 1840–1841, Marcus Morton; 1841–1843, John Davis; 1843–1844, Marcus Morton; 1844–1851, George N. Briggs; 1851–1853, George S. Boutwell; 1853–1854, John H. Clifford; 1854–1855, Emory Washburn; 1855–1858, Henry J. Gardner; 1858–1861, Nathaniel P. Banks; 1861–1866, John A. Andrew; 1866–1869, Alexander H. Bullock; 1869–1872, William Claflin; 1872–1874, William B. Washburn; 1875–1876, William Gaston; 1876–1879, Alexander H. Rice; 1879–1880, Thomas Talbot; 1880–1883, John D. Long.

INDEX OF NAMES

Milton Keynes UK
Ingram Content Group UK Ltd.
UKHW040041281223
435071UK00008B/734

9 789354 013768